From a Sussex Garden

With 'Rose Green'

HC Johnston

First published in 2020, HC Johnston

ISBN-9798682171507

Cover design by: hejo

The Oscars speech:

My thanks go to Laura Bradbear, editor of Sussex Views, who generously allows me to express my gardening opinions all over her nice magazine.

Thanks also to my parents, my sister, her family, and my cousin, for letting me use their gardens as experimental plots, nursery beds and filching areas.

'Rose Green' is my garden writing name, taken from the location of Garden Four. My official name is HC Johnston, and you may find my other writing, such as short stories, under that name.

"Civilization begins with a rose. A rose is a rose is a rose is a rose. It continues with blooming and it fastens clearly upon excellent examples."

Gertrude Stein, As Fine as Melanctha

Foreword

On the general principle that you write the book you cannot find in the bookshops (or on Amazon), this is the book I wish someone had give me when I started out umpteen years ago. (Hands up – over forty).

Parts of this book have appeared as monthly articles in Sussex Views magazine, which I started to write in 2014. I base these on my experience in my gardens in London and Sussex, and those of patient relatives. I am a single-handed gardener; my mistakes are my own.

Many gardening books are full of plants, but gardens need to be full of people. You will find lists of trees and flowers, but also how to make your outdoor space work for your own needs, budget, and time available. And to have fun doing it.

But above all, this book aims to encourage a more positive approach to the space around your home than growing a nice patch of concrete. Even better, it's entirely possible without a slipping a disc.

How to use this book

You can, of course, begin at the beginning and go on to the end, but you can skip through by topic, from what looks good in February to thoughts about style, and maybe some ideas about benches and statues.

You don't have to absorb everything all at once, and you don't have to work through step by step. Anything that delays you from getting into the garden and trying stuff out, or provides an excuse for not taking a decision, should be kicked into touch now.

Start simple, or with the urgent jobs, or the tasks you feel up to, and work in the rest as you go along. This is a craft: there are conventions and habits but, at the core, very few rules.

The only rule is to preserve and enhance life in your garden, whether your own, the plants, or visitors, animal and human (and even relatives).

Where are the pictures?

This book contains references to hundred of plants and garden features and would be impossibly thick and difficult to use if all of them were illustrated in the text.

I strongly suggest, if you are unfamiliar with a plant, that you look up an image on a comprehensive website such as the RHS Plant Finder. But note that professional photographers are concerned with the 'best' picture, not always with recording growing habits and conditions.

To keep a note for yourself, a mobile phone photo will be fine, for your record of your own garden or when visiting other gardens.

We are in danger of 'planting for the photograph'. Please try to choose plants after seeing them growing in a garden, not just from an illustration or catalogue. One gardener's 'dainty' is another gardener's 'insignificant'.

And gardening is not only about the look. Some people like the smell of hawthorn or lilies, some can't abide them. Never underestimate thorns, prickles or stings. Furry plants can be fun. Or grow something scrubby and unlovely purely for its wonderful scent.

Gardens can be for all your senses.

Begin at the beginning –

Gardening: a great British art form.

Over two-thirds of UK homes have a garden of some description. Even if you have no garden, you may have a balcony, yard or open space where a plant can grow.

However, if you are like most of the population, the main impetus behind starting to garden is necessity. Your home, or your parents' home, comes with a patch of ground which is supposed to look nice and not attract rats.

A gardening book needs to recognise that for first-timers, this can feel very scary and alien. To take responsibility for a bunch of green stuff, when knowing little or nothing about it, may be like doing your tax return for the first time. What if everything goes horribly wrong? What if the neighbours complain? *Will this be yet another reason for my in-laws to regard me as a failure?*

Fear begets paralysis or panic. When New Gardener faces First Garden, do you ignore the green stuff - and discover just how quickly things grow and keep growing? Or slash everything back - and discover just how quickly green stuff can turn all brown and withered? (Here's a clue. You can't just ignore or shred a tax return, either).

Help is at hand. Unlike completing your tax return, gardening is a craft skill. You can learn how to garden, you don't need to come from a long line of horny-handed sons of toil (or fey upper-class types with inherited estates).

But you will need some patience, because crafts are absorbed by both mind and hand. They also need some study and, not least, trial and error. Gardening is a mixture of science, art and experience. Books and the media can hand on knowledge and show examples of the art, but they cannot inject instant experience.

Be prepared to get things wrong a few times. Nobody knows how to drive a car the first time they get into one, either. So that expensive palm thingy died? Learn to shrug. There are not many rules in gardening, but here are seven basic ideas to get your mind around:

Seven basic ideas

- Above all, recognise that a garden is a living system.
- Because a garden is full of living things (before you have planted a single seed or laid one paving slab) and these have not always read the book about how they are supposed to behave, gardens can spring surprises.Gardeners must be willing to accept change, because gardens do and will.
- The rhythms of plant life and death are particular, very different from those of animals, and *not intended as a personal criticism of the gardener*.
- Living plants cannot be bullied into growth or flower.
- Quick fixes' are at best liable to be expensive, at worst an expensive disappointment.
- The only plants that do not change their shape, colour or size over the seasons and years are dead. Or plastic.

Take your time. This is not an exam, or a race. There are no garden taste police: if you want gnomes and a huge marble fountain in your thirties semi, have them.

The garden may not be yours. Your gran may need a hand or your son or daughter may have their first property. You may have taken on a churchyard or a piece of roadside verge.

Perhaps you have suddenly been left in charge of the green space attached to a school, hospital, hotel or pub. The principle is the same, to achieve maximum pleasure for the level of effort you are prepared to make.

Whose garden is it, anyway?

Why your garden is not a TARDIS

There is an idea about that, if a garden is an 'outdoor room', somehow a huge number of functions can be rammed into a tiny space. I have seen plans for small gardens with the sandbox beside the vegetable patch beside the barbecue beside the shed, all in a space no larger than a largish living room. The only result here, is surely tears.

If you have a young family, of course they need somewhere to play. So don't expect balls, sand, plastic toys and half-eaten biscuits NOT to end up all over the dahlias. The only way to keep a small child and their little tornado of chaos out of an 'adult relaxing space' is to build a wall, which is a miserable way to use a garden.

Spaces can have many functions if they are well planned, but there is no miracle way to have a pristine terrace for the sundown G&T's at one end and a children's playground at the other, in five metres square.

A lot of gardeners put up with the mess until the family gets a little older, when it starts to make sense to think about a garden for adults. But whatever space you have will probably never be enough for everything you want - the swimming pool, the gym, the sauna, the trotting ring for the ponies – and that means making choices. And probably, upsetting someone, for a while.

Art never comes without sacrifice.

Own the space

Life, as Tom Lehrer said, is like a sewer: "What you get out of it, depends on what you put into it." The only person who really knows what you want out of your garden, and how you can look after it, is you.

Even if you outsource all the heavy work and have a gardener who comes in once or twice a week, the design and mood have to be yours; or else you will only ever be a bystander in your own garden.

So, time spent on planning is rarely wasted. How much time/energy do you foresee giving to your garden?

Now, try again and be realistic. And - Money.

Ah, yes. Also, set a financial budget. (Garden centre owners, cover your eyes now). Your garden will cost something, but need not break the bank. Many useful plants may be available as clumps from the gardens of friends or relatives, and not every tool or garden feature has to be brand spanking new.

Rules of (green) thumb: Structural thinking

The lists and suggestions in the book cover both 'common' plants and more exotic choices, but not necessarily the latest or most fashionable. That's up to you and your budget. But the plants will all grow under most UK circumstances, and can be designed into a variety of garden styles.

Let us consider 'green structure'. As Beth Chatto and other writers point out, leaves last for six months or more, flowers for about three weeks if you're lucky (and many are a lot more fleeting).

Grass, trees and evergreens are the basis of your garden experience through the seasons. Then you can place the more temporary - but vital – features of flowers,scent, texture, and transient leaf colour.

- Of your trees and big structural plants, excluding the lawn, about a third should be evergreen.
- Of these, the majority should be plain, not variegated, as too much yellow splashing looks both artificial and hectic.
- Less than one third evergreens, and the garden will look skimpy, especially in winter.
- Many more evergreens than this begins to approach the style of a public crematorium, which I suspect is not the intention in a private garden.

It is helpful to understand how a plant will fit in, and the amount of upkeep it needs, before dashing out and spending a lot of money. But your garden won't mean much to you unless there is also room for all your favourite flowers, the gifts from your family and friends, the plants that stir your memory and the ones that are playful as well as aesthetic.

Squirting cucumber, anyone? Or the world's hottest chili? Or a really, really, seriously big marrow - Now's the time to make your wish-list, and let it be as bold as you like.

The core plant list

Robin Lane Fox, a well-known garden writer, has a saying, 'Grow what you like, and grow plenty of it.' I agree but amend this slightly to 'Grow what likes you, and grow plenty of it.'

A garden looks happy and contented if plants are growing well, without disease, and are flowering and fruiting freely. A well-arranged garden full of robust, if common, plants looks much more impressive than a patch full of expensive invalids.

Many top-rank garden designers will primarily use 'ordinary' plants – because they are tough and adaptable. The best way to see the plants that will like you is in the gardens of your neighbours. Learn from their mistakes.

If they grow camellias and rhododendrons, but the leaves are a nasty shade of yellow, then the soil is not acid enough for these plants to be comfortable: I'll explain the acid soil thing later. If their fashionable and expensive pieris and skimmia bushes look miserable, again the problem is trying to grow plants which suit damp, mild, acid conditions as found in Cornwall, Wales or the West of Scotland, in an area which is none of those things.

If nothing in their garden is much over two metres tall, or trees are blasted into a truly weird lopsided shape because of the prevailing wind coming off the hills or the coast, then woodland gardens are off the list, until and unless you create a protected dell behind a windbreak.

If you are surrounded by wonderful rhodies and terrific autumn colour, but there is an odd absence of roses, you are probably in Cornwall, where the acid granite or serpentine soils are too poor for them. The hydrangeas will be really bright blue, however – as long as they are somewhere dampish.

This is not a recipe for conservatism. Just because nobody else grows a plant, and you have checked that this is not because of some obvious soil or climate factor, by all means have a go. Not everything will succeed. That's okay.

But, it's a nice day, the garden centre is open, so –

If you're just itching to go shopping RIGHT NOW, here's a list of suggestions, laid out by the month when the plant or flower looks at its best. The list starts with plants that look good in September, because most of us (I hope) can muster a few daffodils and roses earlier in the year, but having a good show later on takes some planning.

I've put evergreens at the end, as these are permanent features and you need to consider them as twelve-month plants. Off we go -

September

Rudbeckia ('Black Eyed Susan', 'Coneflower')

Bright, almost fierce yellow, these daisies vary in height from about a foot for the annuals, which only live for a year, or short-lived perennials, living three to four years, to about six feet/2m for the deep-rooted prairie types like Rudbeckia nitida.

Annuals can come in shades of brown, rust or orange mixed with yellow, but perennials are always yellow. The contrasting 'cone' at the centre of the flower may be black, brown or green, according to variety.

The best-known varieties are 'Goldsturm' and 'Goldquelle' (double-flowered) but the Americans and Germans are breeding new ones all the time. They like sun and a light soil, preferably a light clay.

Dahlia (Tuber, not hardy)

Today we have a wide range of short-growing patio varieties as well as traditional four-foot/1.2m show dahlias: the flowers themselves are described as pom-poms, single, collarette, anemone-flowered, cactus, or decorative. Only worry about that if you're competing in a flower show, otherwise choose what you like.

New varieties are released to the market all the time, although heritage types are still around. 'Bishop of Llandaff' has dark, deeply cut leaves and a brilliant crimson flower, and has now been developed into a range of colours called the 'Bishop's Children' series.

Single flowers are better for insects, such as the spidery 'Honka' types. I also like the Twynings varieties, all named after confectionery brands. 'Twynings After Eight' has white flowers on dark leaves.

Dahlia tubers need to be planted in pots in warmth, preferably in a heated greenhouse, in spring (March/April) or they will not grow big enough to flower by summer. They are greedy for water and feed. In a warm spot you may be able to leave them in the ground over winter, or you can buy new tubers in spring. Dahlias do not survive frost.

Colchicum (Autumn crocus) (Bulb)

These are not, repeat not, related to the garden crocus that appears in spring. An even more misleading name, Meadow Saffron, might suggest they could be used in cooking when they are, in fact, highly poisonous.

Their flowers are in clusters, each up to 7 cm/3 inches or so long, in shades of pinkish-mauve, white or lilac. The bulbs are also large, about three to four inches/10 cm but soft, so be careful when digging around them.

Colchicums flower from the end of August through to November, and come into the garden centres from about August. The bulb will put up flowers just sitting on a windowsill, but unless planted in the garden, will then die afterwards. Their other common name, Naked Ladies, is because the flowers are produced before the leaves.

The leaves get their own back in spring. Think of a big fat daffodil leaf, 40cm/15 inches long and usually a couple of inches/3-4 cm wide, broad and fleshy. Although the flower may look pretty at the front of a border, the leaves will not. Place them behind other plants for spring effect, or under spring-flowering shrubs. Bulbs are not cheap, so study your types first.

The main types available in garden centres are Colchicum speciosus, 'Waterlily' (double), and 'The Giant', but there are about a dozen species available from specialist nurseries.

October

Chrysanthemum (officially, dendranthemum)

Traditional chrysanthemums come in shades of red, yellow, orange and rust, and in lilacs and maroons as well. Their flower shape may be a pom-pom, or single, or anemone-type, double, shaggy or globular. Their petals may be flat, quilled, fringed or spoon-shaped. Some are a foot/30cm tall, others reach four feet/1.2m with ease. Some get through winter, but many only survive if protected in a greenhouse.

Start off cuttings, which you can buy mail-order, in spring, taking out the top so they branch out, and plant out in about end April. Dig them up after flowering in November, and put in pots for the winter.

There are some truly hardy garden types. These have small flowers but lots of them, about an inch/2 cm across, and specialist nurseries stock them. Look out for 'Bronze Elegance', 'Dr Tom Parr' (brownish), 'Anastasia' and 'Mei-kyo' (both pink), all about 15 inches/40 cm tall. In a warm position with light soil, these spread. You may also find the singles, pink 'Clara Curtis' or 'Duchess of Edinburgh, and the old 'Emperor of China', although these can be rather lanky. 'Ruby Mound' is a good doer.

The new ranges of patio chrysanths are derived from Korean chrysanthemums and will probably survive most winters in a warm, dryish spot, but as a group they are too new to be certain.

Nerine (Bulb)

In September you may spot really, really bright pink flowers about 60 cm/2 feet tall, looking like bunched-up spidery lilies. These are nerines, usually Nerine bowdenii, and they need heat, which is why you see them under south-facing walls.

If happy, they clump up fast. Their leaves come out in spring but wither away before flowering, so remember where they are. Buy them as tubers in late spring.

November

Michaelmas daisy (Aster, of gardens)

These mainly come from North America, with some Mediterranean blood. Look for a variety which is 'novae-angliae' or 'New England', or 'frikartii' varieties as these resist mildew. Good varieties are 'Alma Potchske' (bright cerise), 'Monch' (lavender) and 'Violette' (purple).

Most start flowering in September but many carry on almost to December. Dwarf or window-box types like 'dumosus' are not as robust.

The old nova-belgii ('New York') types like 'Winston Churchill' need a lot of spraying with fungicide although some, like 'Little Carlow', seem tougher. You must also remember to divide the plants in spring.

New varieties are being introduced, often as bedding plants, but how perennial they are is uncertain. Wild types like 'divaricatus' or 'ericoides' are strong-growing but not big-flowered: their flowers are attractive in the mass, as pastel-shaded clouds and drifts.

The scientific re-namers have been at the daisies but I suspect the new botanical names will be roundly ignored by the nursery trade, so just ask for 'aster' or Michaelmas daisy.

Berries In a small garden

it is hardly worth growing a plant solely for berries: they must offer some other quality as well, whether of shape, leaf or flower. Three families of plants are berry favourites: pyracantha, cotoneaster and sorbus (rowans).

Others that produce a good but less spectacular berry crop include hawthorn, berberis and viburnum, plus ornamental crab-apples (malus) and grapes (vitis). I am assuming that you will take the elderberries and blackberries for your own use. Pyracantha (firethorn) is usually sold as a hedge or wall shrub, as it responds well to clipping (after the berries, of course).

Pyracantha can be grown as a free-standing shrub, or even a small tree. My specimen in Garden Three was about forty years old, six metres/ twenty feet high and across, and looked like a huge white cloud when flowering in June. Varieties include 'Navaho'. ('Mohave', commonly sold, is not very disease resistant).

Cotoneasters (Co-tone-ee-aster, please, no cotton-easters) can be evergreen or deciduous. As the last turn very bright colours in autumn, the loss of leaves is not such a disadvantage.

There are dozens of types which come in a variety of leaf shape and colour, from large and lance-shaped in light sage green (salicifolia) to small, dark and glossy. Be aware that their berries were designed by Nature to make little cotoneasters. All can be ferocious seeders.

Rowans are small trees and some are described in the 'Trees, please' section.

December

Holly (Ilex) (Evergreen)

Holly is a slow-growing plant when young, but like other shrubs that take a while to get into their stride, can appear to mark time for a couple of years, only to grow at about a foot/30 cm a year or more thereafter.

Most hollies will eventually grow between ten and twenty feet high (3-7 metres) and as much around, if not pruned into a standard tree by gradually removing the lower branches. They must be regarded as large permanent features and placed accordingly.

Variegated versions include 'Golden King' and 'Silver Queen', and some varieties are much less prickly than others e.g. Ilex camellifolia. Common holly does make a good hedge, but clearing up the dead or cut leaves is a job for someone else.

Ivy (Hedera helix) (Evergreen)

Ivy is only a climbing plant while juvenile. When high enough up the host tree, it reached maturity and starts to flower and produce berries, and changes habit to a branched shrub.

If cuttings are taken of this shrub form, usually identified as 'arborea', they never climb but remain as bushes, and these can sometimes be found on sale. If you want a bush, fine, but if you thought you were buying a climber, not so good, so take note.

Small-leaved ivies are available in a wide rage of shapes, ruffles and variegation, and even the small sizes sold for winter flowerboxes or as houseplants will grow in the garden.

Large-leaved ivies are more tender. ‘Marengo’ and ‘Sulphur Heart’ are variegated forms of the Canary Islands ivy and ‘Hibernica’, or Irish ivy, is plain green. They grow rampantly but can get caught by frost.

January

Bergenia (Evergreen)

Also called elephants' ears. Large leathery leaves about 10-20 cm long, with stout rhubarb-like stalks of pink flowers in early spring, from February/March.

The common one is indestructible. There are a lot of German varieties, such as the ones named after composers e.g. 'Beethoven' and they have larger flowers. 'Silberlicht' is a popular white variety and 'purpurea' is bright magenta.

Easily split apart to make more and makes good ground cover and edging, such as for a drive, but the fancier types need reasonable soil as well. Some find the plant clumsy-looking but I think it is bold.

Winter jasmine (Jasminum nudiflorum) (Evergreen)

Evergreen, sprawling, with yellow flowers in January and February. Can be cut back into shape, or will get several metres high and across. Note there is no scent.

I'm not as keen on this as some, as it can make an untidy hummock with not much in its favour for eleven months of the year. But as you can clip it to Kingdom Come, this is another possible hedge.

February

Christmas Rose (Hellebore) (Evergreen)

The white Christmas rose (Helleborus niger) is not an easy plant to please, so these days you will normally find white versions of Helleborus orientalis, also called the Lenten Rose, on offer instead.

Other orientalis types are available in pale yellow and greens as well as traditional pinkish and purple shades, and some approach black. Varieties with freckles and spots at the centre may be called 'guttatus'. A lot are seed-raised these days, like the 'Harvington' strain. Double flowers are currently popular.

Of the species, look out for Helleborus argutifolius, which likes sun and offers big heads of lime green flowers in late spring. This will seed around, and grows to about a metre across. A word of warning: all hellebores are poisonous, so wash your hands after splitting, cutting or propagating them.

Christmas cowslip (Pulmonaria rubra) (Evergreen)

The Christmas Cowslip has red bell-shaped flowers, from pinkish red to a clear coral according to the variety. On my plants these start appearing in November and carryon until March. The variety I grow is 'Redstart', a bright coral variety that has a well-deserved RHS Award of Garden Merit. Acts as robust ground-cover when not in flower. Sun or shade seems to suit it equally.

Snowdrops (Galanthus) (Bulb)

In some gardens snowdrops become weeds, in others (like three of mine) they take one look at the conditions and promptly die. Although snowdrops are bulbs, they like a lot of moisture and they do noticeably better in the cooler, damper North than the south of England.

Snowdrops, like many of our garden bulbs, come from Turkey, the Middle East and southern Russia. Many of the old named varieties are rumoured to have been brought back by soldiers from the Crimea, a piece of living history. Because they cannot survive dryness for long, snowdrops are better bought, or lifted from a friendly neighbour, as growing plants than dry bulbs.

If you do buy them dry, as with all pre-packed bulbs, check to make sure that they have not been collected in the wild. This should be stated unequivocally on the pack. If the description only says 'Packed in Holland', leave them. This does not say how the bulbs were obtained, and some are being ‘collected’ to extinction.

The ordinary snowdrop, Galanthus nivalis, may suffice for most purposes, but the double version is very pretty, a frilly little flower stuffed to bursting with green and white petals, and no more difficult than the ordinary one.

There is another rather frail native, the so-called Northumbrian snowdrop, which has yellow markings instead of green on the petal, but this is much trickier to keep, and very expensive.

Or you can venture into the world of named varieties. If you see 'Atkinsii', 'Magnet', 'Straffan' or 'Sam Arnott', take a deep breath at the price but they are often much bigger, at six to eight inches/20 cm tall, and showier. Collectors spend six to eight pounds a bulb for rarer sorts and over £20 for … I’ve lost you, haven’t I.

March

Daffodil (Narcissus) (Bulb)

Daffodils fall into the group of bulbs that appreciate a lot of moisture. They are plants of alpine meadows and mountains in their native lands, which are Spain, Portugal, southern France, Italy and Greece.

Although these are warm countries, altitude and the effect of snow-melt in natural conditions mean that these bulbs grow both cool and moist in spring. Note that dry bulbs come into the garden centres in August and prefer to be planted then as well.

Botanically, all daffodils belong to the narcissus family.

Nobody knows whether our 'native' Lent Lily or Tenby Daffodil, Pseudonarcissus obvallaris, is actually a native or some ancient introduction, but it is noticeably happier in the wetter West than the dry East.

For general garden show, the so-called dwarf daffodils are more weatherproof and a better bet than tall ones, dwarf meaning up to fifteen inches/40 cm tall, so not insignificant. These multiply rapidly, cut well, and produce at least as good a pool of colour as their larger relatives.

Try 'Jack Snipe', 'February Gold', 'Tete a Tete', 'Jetfire', 'Pepper' (orange), 'Thalia' (white), 'Hawera', 'February Silver' (white) and 'Pipit'. 'Rip van Winkle' is a little double yellow, as is 'Pencrebar'.

Of the taller sorts, 'Geranium', 'White Lion' (double), 'Topolino' (lemon), 'Ice Follies' (white) 'Golden Ducat' and 'Kesteven' (yellow) are all reliable. 'Ice Follies' grows so fast the bulbs are cropped for the drug galanthamine. I cannot find any virtue in the split-corona or 'Orchid' varieties.

Later on, the gardener's narcissus group, which includes 'Cheerfulness' (yellow or white), the 'Poets' Narcissus', 'Actaea' and their double versions, are as desirable for their scent as their flower. These like warmer, drier conditions than daffodils. If happy they will naturalise freely.

And don't throw out the 'Paperwhite' or 'Solidor' that you bought for Christmas flowering. In a warm, dry, sheltered spot, they will take to life outdoors without difficulty.

As daffodil bulbs bulk up, they may crowd each other so flowers are no longer formed, or the buds turn dry and brown. The simple answer is to divide them regularly, after flowering, every four years or so. If you lift bulbs, replant them by August as daffodils and narcissi start into growth very early.

Forsythia

Most of the year a forsythia bush is not a great asset. The growth is sprawling, the leaves are undistinguished, and it has no winter value. But for a few weeks in spring, a well-grown forsythia is a huge firework explosion of gold.

The trick is not so much in the variety - although 'Beatrix Farrand' is recommended - as how you grow it. When faced with the cat's cradle of an old bush, be bloody, bold and resolute. In spring, chop back to the framework of large branches without mercy.

If the bush is neither senile nor in a hopelessly dark position, it will immediately sprout straight, chestnut-brown, strong branches, up to eight or ten feet/2.5 m long. Cut out oldest branches every year, up to a third of the plant, and you'll have a display to be proud of.

Crocus (Bulb)

Members of the crocus family will, in fact, have been putting their heads above the parapet for a good five months now, but mid-spring is their main season. Crocuses can be white to yellow to near-orange, lavender to deep reddish-purple; they can be striped, feathered or plain. There is one in old pink, and a rarity reputed to be aquamarine.

The main groups of crocuses are the small, early 'chrysanthus' types, the later, large 'Dutch' or 'vernus' crocuses, and the species, such as tommasinianus hybrids ('Tommies')

Chrysanthus crocuses come in delicate shades of white, lavender and yellow: 'Snow Bunting' (white) 'E.A. Bowles' (yellow), 'Blue Pearl' (blue-lavender), 'Cream Beauty' (cream) and 'Ladykiller' (white and purple). They grow to about three inches/6cm high.

Dutch crocuses (vernus types) are much bigger all round and usually only offered by colour, white, lavender, purple or yellow. But by George, they make a splash. See St James' Park in London as an example.

Of the species, some will flower in October and November - such as zonatus - but for spring flowers, keep an eye out for 'Whitewell Purple' and 'Ruby Giant', in deep rich colour, as well as lavender-coloured Crocus tommasinianus.

Many species crocuses come from Greece or Turkey, but have been grown in our gardens for centuries. Crocus angustifolius, the 'Cloth of Gold' crocus, is yellow feathered with brown. Crocus ancyrensis or 'Golden Bunch' comes from near Ankara in Turkey. Crocus atticus and sieberi, in white and purples, are worth a try. Crocuses are trouble-free, except when eaten by mice or squirrels, so plant them deep.

April

Tulip (Bulb)

The tulip has a long aristocratic pedigree and an everlasting place in financial history. The bulb that hit the jackpot in the 'Tulip Mania' of the seventeenth century, 'Semper Augustus', is still around, a yellow and red striped flower which at one point traded for the price of an Amsterdam town-house. 'Keiserkroon' is similar ('King's Crown') and of eighteenth-century date.

The real trick with a tulip is not how to flower them the first year, but how to keep them thereafter. The parents of garden tulips come from high mountain areas in what is now Iraq and Iran, where winters are freezing and summers are parched.

They do not appreciate constant damp and can easily rot off in heavy soils. One way is to lift the bulbs and keep dry in winter, but the damage done by forking around soft tulip bulbs is often the equal of anything winter can throw at them.

But there are some toughies. 'Apeldoorn' varieties, in red, yellow and red-flushed amber are tall, flower towards the end of April, and are big and bold and what most people imagine when they think of tulips.

Smaller, but still recognisably traditional tulips, are Darwin or Cottage varieties such as 'Queen of the Night' (maroon) and 'Dame Clara Butt' (pink). At a lower level still, varieties like 'Princess Irene' (burnt orange) and 'Keiserkroon' (yellow and red) will carry on from year to year. 'White Emperor', 'Ballerina' and 'Yellow Triumphator' are lily-flowered in style, that is, with long recurved petals, and may also stay more than one season.

Smaller yet, are the species tulips and relatives. Nobody is certain whether 'Marjoletti' is a species or a very ancient garden variety. It has small graceful primrose flowers and grows to about a foot/30cm. The 'lady tulip' is similar, such as 'Lady Jane'. 'Praestans' is a strong vermilion, and bears several flowers to each eight-inch/20cm stem. This characteristic has passed on to yellow-flowered 'Georgette' and other new varieties.

Waterlily tulips, Tulipa kaufmanniana and Tulipa greigii such as 'Red Riding Hood' are often sold as rock garden tulips. The plants are short, no more than eight inches/20 cm tall, but the flowers are huge by comparison. They are striking in red, orange, yellow and white. These like the sharp drainage of a rockery or wall, meaning they will not only stay but multiply.

Clematis

Some of the large-flowered clematis will be starting now, such as 'Nellie Moser'. You may already have had a good show off Clematis montana , which is vigorous, with four-petalled white or pink flowers, or spring specialists like Clematis alpina, which is in lavender shades in a bell-shape.

Where they can be kept damp and shaded, as in the north-west of England, clematis will give a stupendous show. If they dry out, as in most of the south-east, they will tend to collapse with clematis wilt, visible as dry brown shrivelled leaves. This can be kept at bay by using large amounts of fungicide, but that is not the message of this book. Try them on a north wall, or keep them damp.

Anemone (Bulb)

'De Caen' and 'St Brigid' anemones have been bred from several Mediterranean species, and come in bright reds and purples as well as lavender and white. These are the sort sometimes sold as cut flowers. When grown in hot dry positions these will multiply, but as they are untidy plants, are best in the veg garden for cutting, rather than a garden feature.

May

Cranesbill / Herbaceous Geranium

Interesting cut leaves, often evergreen, and five-petalled flowers in white, pink, lavender, magenta or maroon. There is a lot of development at the moment: new varieties like Geranium 'Ann Folkard', 'Patricia', 'Mayflower', 'Sweet Heidi', 'Rozanne', 'Brookside' are all robust.

They can be a mainstay of a landscape garden and are used to effect at Great Comp. A few are evergreen such as Geranium renardii. Be careful of the 'Mourning Widow' or Geranium phaeum, as in my experience it is a bothersome seeder. But some people are fascinated by the deep maroon flowers. There is a pretty white version

After flowering, you can chop the taller versions off just above ground. They will grow new leaves to look respectable for the rest of the year and some many even produce more flowers.

Border and Siberian Iris (Evergreen)

The iris family is enormous, covering everything from bulbs (Iris reticulata) to border plants ('German' iris) to water plants (Iris japonica) and from all types of climate from desert (onocyclus irises) to sub-tropical (Iris tectorum). They can be tiny, as in Iris pumila at 5 cm, or 2 metre giants, as in Iris spuria. The main non-bulb types grown in English gardens are the border or German irises and Iris sibirica.

Border irises are very ancient.

Iris pallida (lavender) and Iris germanica (purple) types have been in cultivation for many centuries: some are used in perfume-making ('orris' or Iris florentina). They grow from an exposed tuber on the surface and need sharp drainage. White irises are frequently planted in Muslim cemeteries.

The other ancient sort is Iris variegata, where the petals that stand up, the standards, are yellow but the petals that drop down, the falls, are chestnut brown.

These old stagers are very tough and, if a neighbour or relative offers you a clump, are a good place to start. The flowers are not as big as the fancier types but that makes them more weather-proof. They will spread into good clumps quickly. There are thousands of varieties on the market but here is a brief list.

Lavender blue: 'Jane Phillips', Iris pallida

White: 'Frosted Flame', 'White City'
Edged violet (plicata): 'Blue Shimmer','Dancer's Veil'
Purple: Iris germanica, 'Blue Rhythm','Braithwaite'
Yellow: 'Ole Kala', 'Berkeley Gold', 'Rajah'
Peach, bronze: 'Party Dress', 'Rocket', 'Kent Pride', 'Provencal'

Siberian irises have deep violet, rather spidery flowers and their leaves are like a clump of rushes. They like damper conditions but are also spreaders.

There are some different colours around, although I like the basic version: if you wish you could have white, 'White Swirl', or paler blue-violet 'Cambridge' or even mauve 'Sparkling Rose'.

I also grow Californian irises (Iris innominata) which I think of as the Chelsea iris as they come out in May. These are sprawlers, and like both warmth and some dampness.

They come in white, cream, yellow, lavender or purple, and some bronzy/pinkish shades. I can recommend 'Mitre', a strong purple, but all are pretty. Some people find them trickier than the others.

June

Roses

The pro's and con's of the rose question are dealt with in more detail in a separate chapter.

Lilac (Syringa)

Not hugely fashionable at the moment, most varieties are now over a century old. The most popular double white is 'Madame Lemoine'. Others include 'Louis Spaeth' (purple) and 'Primrose' (truthfully, a deep cream). There has been a lot of development in Poland and Russia, so good plants may have (to us) strange names. Look out for 'Old Moscow' and similar varieties. Lilacs in the more delicate looking 'microphylla' group are pinker but have smaller flowers, such as 'Palibin'.

Lilac suckers vigorously, which can be a problem if uncontrolled. The bush can be pruned heavily but does not take very well to shaping. After flowering, lilac has distinctive but not particularly attractive foliage.

As the bush has an open habit, lilac is ideal as a framework for growing other, lightly-built, climbing plants such as viticella clematis, or annuals such as morning glories. I grew a golden-leaved type but it tends to scorch in sun.

July

Bush mallow (Lavatera olbia)

In July look around. There will be a lot of big bushes with very vivid pink flowers. These, if the flowers are big, pink and circular, made up of six or eight petals, are Lavatera. If the bush is particularly big and pink, this is almost certainly Lavatera olbia, which is the closest the British garden can get to an instant shrub.

Lavatera are also very easy to strike from cuttings, which is how so many types have been introduced so rapidly over the last few years. Colours range from white to burgundy. Place them with room to spread but out of the wind as they blow about and break.

St Johns' Wort/Rose of Sharon (Hypericum)

The St John's Wort family includes pretty alpines (Hypericum olympicum), vigorous ground cover (Hypericum calycinum, the Rose of Sharon), shrubs and herbaceous types.

The star of the show in July is undoubtedly the shrubby Hypericum 'Hidcote'. This will become a dome some three or four feet / 1.2m across within a year or two of planting, covered in midsummer with golden, five-petalled tassel-centred flowers somewhat like a rose, which may continue on into September.

In the same vein but more tender is 'Rowallane', which shows a more fragile nature by frequently dying to the ground in winter, like a fuchsia. The flowers are even larger and even brighter to make up for this, however.

So what's the catch? All hypericums are susceptible to a rust disease, seen as orange spots on the leaves. Although not normally a killer, this is unsightly, and some clones are more at risk than others.

The simplest advice is not to buy disease in, and to make sure that when you do prune your bushes (on the principle of cutting out one branch in three in spring) that the prunings are kept well away from other plants.

Buddleia

Buddleia can look a mess, if not tidied up from time to time. Like most fast-growing plants, it will grow more in a season than it can support, leaving dead branches all over for next summer. The dead flowers are not attractive and will spray seeds right, left and centre. Buddleia loses some but not all leaves in winter and can look very scraggy indeed, as the bush lacks shape.

Buddleia, therefore, needs a degree of care and attention. In spring, take out the dead wood, take out the old branches, one in three. Take off the dead flowers when they are over. If the naked flowerless bush offends your eye, grow an annual climber through.

Good varieties include 'Black Knight' (dark purple), 'Lochinch' (lavender, my favourite) and there are now some good pink shades. I have found the 'dwarf' types and Nanho varieties not robust enough in the garden.

Utterly different is Buddleia globosa, the orange ball buddleia, which will grow into a small tree. The leaves are dark green, setting off the orange flowers in a striking way. There are some crosses between orange and purple types, but most are a good argument for leaving well enough alone.

The plant is named after Dr Buddle, and in usual manner in the nineteenth century, a Latin 'ia' was added to his name, as also Dahl-ia. Now, a 'j' is sometimes added, although the doctor's name is not Buddlej, nor did the Romans have a J in their alphabet.

So 'buddleia' it stays, for me.

Not buddl-jar.

August

Fuchsia

Most fuchsias come from Latin America, the main garden varieties grown in the UK deriving from species found in Peru and Bolivia. Depending on how high up the Andes they grow, they may be hardy, or not. The soft-growing types used in hanging baskets are usually not. The hardy or bush fuchsias may have small flowers but lots of them, or fewer but more glamorous flowers.

As is usual in the garden, small-flowered varieties are normally hardier than those with big fat flowers.

For permanent planting as bushes or hedges, Fuchsia magellanica types are unequalled. These grow to 3-4 feet /1-1.3 m and make up the fuchsia hedges you will see in Ireland or the West Country. They have whippy but profuse growth, small dark leaves, and slender flowers in red and purple. The berries that form in the autumn are edible, incidentally, and can be made into jam.

Coloured-leaved varieties are notable such as Fuchsia magellanica aurea with gold leaves, and Fuchsia magellanica versicolor, whose leaves mix grey-green, pinkish and white. A bright white-variegated version with white flowers is called 'Sharpitor'.

Fuchsia riccartonii has slightly larger red/purple flowers. 'Hawkshead' has small white flowers. 'Lady Bacon' is very tall at 2 metres, with many small flowers in red, white and (almost) blue.

For bigger flowers, 'Mrs Popple', 'Dollar Princess', 'Brutus' and 'Empress of Prussia' carry on the red and purple theme.

Pink and lavender shades can be found in 'Delta's Sarah', 'Display', 'Prosperity', and 'Chillerton Beauty'.

Flowers in white plus red or pink are 'Checkerboard', 'Alice Hoffman', 'Madame Cornelisson' and 'Snowcap'.

'Genii' has golden leaves and purple and red flowers.

The bigger–flowered types are more tender and may die to the ground every winter. If you want to build up a bigger bush, they will need shelter and warmth, such as a wall, but also some dampness. Fuchsias can be pruned and are long-lived in the right place.

Day lilies (Hemerocallis)

The old double variety that may be in your granny's garden is a Japanese plant known as 'Kwanso Flore Pleno'. She grew it because it is indestructible. The flower is lily-shaped, in a rusty orange, sometimes with a maroon flush at the base. I've turfed most of mine out: loads of long strappy leaves, very few flowers. But your Chinese friends may appreciate a plant; these are the 'lily buds' of Chinese cuisine.

The majority of decorative, modern day lilies grow to just under a metre and although each flower does only last a day, these are produced in succession.

Dwarf, yellow: 'Corky', 'Stella d'Oro',

'Golden Chimes'. Dwarf, other: 'Little Wine Cup' (mulberry) Standard, yellow: 'Marion Vaughn',

'Double River Wye' (double), 'Hyperion' Standard, maroon/red: 'Stafford', 'Autumn Red',

'Berlin Red' Standard, pink/peach: 'Pink Damask',

'Stoke Poges' Standard, bi-coloured: 'Frans Hals'

Species: all yellow and have a sweet lily-like scent.

Flava, a.k.a. lilioasphodelus

Citrina, nocturnal

Altissima, tall.

Montbretia (Crocosmia) (Bulb)

Officially called crocosmia these days, these are the orange-red-yellow flowers that look like little lilies and flower in August and September. Anything from 20cm to 1 metre tall. They like some damp in the soil and will take some shade.

Look out for 'Lucifer', 'Emily Mackenzie' and 'George Davison'. If you have too many clumps of the common montbretia, note you can't just chuck these over the fence as this is now categorised as an invasive plant and this is no longer allowed.

Evergreens

Essential, but not overwhelming

A good rule of thumb is to aim for one third of your shrubs and smaller plants to be evergreen. If you get to more than half, the garden can look 'heavy' or somewhat municipal.

Most of us have some evergreens (such as the lawn, for starters), and they can be sure-fire sellers: evergreen is a 'magic word' in the nursery trade. When you wander about on New Year's Day, glass of Hogmanay whisky in hand, the plants that give form to your garden will largely be the evergreens. Unless you don't have any, in which case it will look brown and twiggy.

In the UK, we have some native evergreen shrubs and trees, but not many: holly, ivy, yew, pine, box (buxus) and juniper, for the record. Most garden evergreen trees and shrubs either come from very much hotter places, like the Med and Australia, or very much colder ones, like the Rocky Mountains or the Alps. As a result, not all of them like the cold, some can't stand damp winters, and some get scorched by wind.

And although evergreen leaves don't all drop off in autumn, they can drop in summer; eucalyptus, for one. Because leaves last longer than a year, if they get blasted or cut or damaged, you're got a tatty plant until new ones grow in.

Conifers are useful but not faultless. Noble when given space, many will not grow back if pruned, leaving a dead patch and a misshapen plant. Some sprout ('revert') out of control.

'Dwarf' conifers are often just slower-growing: the Sir Harold Hillier Garden at Romsey has some huge examples, which were cute when they were babies but are now 4 metre/20 foot adults. Our coastal winds can knock conifers about even if the gardener does not.

But, every garden needs evergreens. So, thinking more widely, here are some toughies that look good and avoid the 'half-dead dwarf conifer' syndrome.

Evergreen trees (over 3 metres /10 feet)

Trees cast shade, and big evergreen trees cast a lot of shade, so use with care. Very little will grow under a tree that casts permanent shade.

Bay tree (Laurus nobilis) will grow to 25ft/6m. Likes sun. This is the sort you cook with. Or make into a crown for a Caesar or a poet.

Holly (Ilex): look at large types like Highclere hollies (Ilex altaclarensis) which have big, polished smooth leaves, as well as variegated types. Also to 25ft/6m. Doesn't mind shade.

Eucalyptus are very handsome and very, very fast but they shed their leaves in June, and these are hard and do not rot easily, so place carefully. They also take up a lot of water. Many types are now available so be careful you don't pick a giant.

Portugal laurel (Prunus lusitanica): smaller leaves than hedging laurel and an elegant habit, up to 20ft/5m. Don't try cooking with this or cherry laurel: they're poisonous.

Pittosporum: small neat leaves, in upright, bush or dwarf form, plain, variegated or golden. A New Zealander, graceful, and a coastal speciality. Plain forms include 'Arundel Green' and 'Oliver Twist'. 'Elisabeth' has bright white speckled variegation, and 'Garnettii' has neat white leaf-edges. To 15ft/4m.

Or be bold and plant an **olive** tree. There is a commercial plantation on trial in Essex.

Myrtle and **privet** can get to the 3 metre mark, as can many **bamboos**.

Pines are very handsome and a key plant in Japanese gardens but the forest types can get very scraggy. The more ornamental types such as the Serbian spruce and dwarfer Japanese pines keep to a smaller globular shape. Cedars and cypress trees need their own space.

Evergreen bushes

Our native **Yew** (Taxus baccata), is too large and funereal to be popular in small gardens, but the upright Irish yew Taxus baccata hibernica, is a pretty plant, particularly in the golden version called Aurea. Remember that yew berries are poisonous.

Other larger bushes include:

Cherry laurel (Prunus laurocerasus): the robust laurel of Victorian villa hedges, a large leaf, sometimes with large black berries. Can be pruned back to the trunk but if grown as a hedge, try not to cut the leaves in half, as they look very messy, and give off cyanides when cut (so don't stick prunings in a car and leave them).

Choisya ternata, 'Mexican orange blossom' makes a robust, bushy hedge to 5 feet/1.8 metres and recovers well from cutting back. White flowers in May and again in October. Available in green, gold or narrow-leafed versions such as 'Snow Flurries' or 'Aztec Pearl'. Grows wide but can be kept trimmed. Some people don't like the pungent smell of the leaves.

Eleagnus submacrophylla: the large bush evergreen eleagnus have silvered leaves, which can be seen on young growth even in the variegated versions like 'Gilt Edge' usually grown. These can 'revert' so if you see plain green leaves on a variegated bush, cut the branch out. 'Quicksilver' is smaller-leaved but more tender.

Fatsia japonica: huge, hand-shaped leaves on a rather rangy shrub up to 5 metres, but widely grown for a tropical effect.

Mahonia japonica: a tall shrub with holly-shaped leaflets on a long stem, and spires of sweet-scented yellow flowers in very early spring. Can get big, to10 feet/3 m plus, a back of border plant. Look for 'Charity'.

Olearia dentata: The New Zealand daisy-bush, bunches of white daisy flowers in midsummer, and greyish, holly-like leaves the rest of the year. Up to 3 metres. Can take a decision to die after about 10 years.

Osmanthus delavayi: small-leaved but very shiny, very dark on a neat bush, and white flowers in April. Bush can get to 2 metres.

Spotted laurel (Aucuba): the other 'laurel', normally grown in a golden-spotted or marked variety although the parent plant is plain green. Can be a ray of sunshine in winter if well grown. Bright red berries, sometimes. These can collapse with a mystery fungus disease that turns the leaves black.

Yucca: the Adam's Needles produce clumps of hard grey spiky leaves. They need dry soils and a sunny position or a tub. Come in plain or variegated varieties.

If you have a good flowering type, they will send up 2 metre spires of white bells in late summer. An 'architectural' plant, but painful if you run into one, so place them carefully.

Evergreen shrubs up to 1 metre/3 feet

Euonymus: Nearest thing to a plastic plant. There are OODLES of other evergreens, so go back to the list.

Germander: Teucrium fruticans is a medium-sized bush with grey leaves and pale blue flowers in May, which can be pruned into a hedge. It loves sun and bees love it. Teucrium chamaedrys is a little dark green shrub with dusty cerise flowers in July, which can be kept clipped as a very low hedge, at about 20 cm.

Heathers: Erica, Calluna, Daboecia. These are evergreen but need to be clipped over after flowering to keep them neat. Some will grow on any soil but the glamorous summer-flowering types need acid soil.

Hebe: All the hebes (shrubby veronicas) grown in the UK are evergreen but some are mainly grown for their leaves, which may be grey, bluish, bright or dark green, normally arranged in neat geometric patterns down the branches. The bushes themselves may be a bit humpy. The whipcord hebes such as Armstrongii look like golden conifers.

Lavender (Lavendula): all types are ever-grey, but not very long-lived on damp English soils. They are best on chalk or sand, or in a pot. They come easily from cuttings or seed. You must cut back hard after flowering or the bush gets straggly.

Lonicera: the bush honeysuckle is a small-leaved hedging plant in green or gold ('Baggesen's Gold') which is easy to clip for topiary. Which is just as well because it grows so fast you will need to clip three times a year. Or grow into a bush a metre or two across. Very easy from cuttings.

Sicilian Myrtle (Myrtus communis tarentina): part of every Victorian bride's posy, this myrtle has small dark green leaves, a spicy scent, and little white powder-puffs of flower in August. It does need a warm wall, however.

Privet: not to be despised. The ordinary wild sort is Ligustrum vulgare but the hedging types are usually Ligustrum ovalifolium, which come in green, gold, and variegated white or gold forms. Takes pruning well. Ligustrum lucidum, the Chinese privet, has much larger leaves and will become a small tree.

Rosemary: sprawling plants, even in the 'upright' versions. Greyish green leaves. The variegated forms are called 'gold' and 'silver' but are actually not very effective in the garden, although antique plants. Flowers in April, in white, pink or pale blue: some varieties have royal blue flowers. Look out for 'Green Ginger', named for how it smells.

Sage: In grey, gold–splashed, gold or purple leaved forms, herb sage is a fast growing and effective shrub for a sunny spot and on light soils, but can get mildew in damp winters. Also gets to 2 metres across if it likes you, but you can cut it back.

Santolina: cotton lavender has little silver leaves and is mildly aromatic. There is a green version, Santolina virens, whose smell is quite strong. All need to be trimmed back hard in spring to keep them tight. A new golden-leaved type is called 'Lemon Fizz' and seems quite robust.

For first gardeners

A law of large numbers

The 'grow what likes you and grow plenty of it' point is because many gardens have a very hit and miss look. One specimen might be an accident, two might be a coincidence, but three looks like a design.

Grouping plants that do well into beds or groves has a much greater impact than a single plant, as long as not merely boring or an excuse not to think about what to plant where.

A grove of five white-stemmed birches or a series of beds of iris in separate colours will be more visually effective and deliberate than one here and one there. As will roses grouped into threes and fives, but not corralled into rose–beds. Most rose bushes are not very shapely and the flowers look much better with other planting around them to set them off.

Even in so-called prairie planting, the effect depends on repetition of a limited number of types of plants growing well, not just variety. It may seem a lot of money when you buy three larger plants of the same kind, but the visual payback can be instant.

However, do give your new plants plenty of space to expand because you will not 'remember to cut them back later' or 'take one out if it gets too big'. Nobody ever does.

A note on first tools

Basics: a large fork and spade for digging, stainless steel if you can, stout wooden handles for preference.

A lawn rake, which has long thin wires in a fan-shape.

A garden rake, which has a cross-bar with teeth set along.

A long-handled hoe is useful, either the traditional Dutch hoe with a D-shaped blade, or one with a small, chisel-like blade.

If you have a lawn, a half-moon edger will be handy.

You also need a sharpening stone or strip for this and the spades, because sharp tools do make a difference.

You will need a hand-fork, a hand-trowel, and a pair of secateurs. None of these needs to be stainless steel but plastic forks and trowels are useless unless you garden on sand.

If you have trees and shrubs, a pair of loppers will be needed in winter and early spring. A pruning saw is essential for bigger jobs.

Keep an eye out in charity shops for old tools, because these are often stronger and more durable than modern ones. Ash-handled digging spades and forks are invaluable. A garden rake with teeth made of nails through a metal bar is far stronger than one that is just a piece of bent steel. Relatives may have tools they no longer need, or your local auction room/house clearance store may have some.

A note on gardener's Latin

Why do plants have difficult names? In this book, where possible I have given both the 'common' name (like daffodil) as well as the botanical name (Narcissus). This is for a very good reason.

'Common' names may not exist if a plant is not common, or not native. There is no common name for a dahlia. The plants come from Mexico and the European scientist who named them decided to commemorate Dr Dahl, a Swedish botanist. There is never any outcry that 'dahlia' is somehow 'too difficult' because we are used to it, now.

Plants have two official names, rather like people. The family name is put first and has a capital letter, and the describer name comes second and does not have a capital. They are in a sort of Latin-cum-Greek, because these were the languages all Western scientists used when the systems for naming were set up in the eighteenth century.

These two names act as unique identifiers. The same two names will identify the same plant in any country in the world, to any gardener. If the plant were a car, then Ford is the family name, Mondeo is the describer.

Rosa rugosa, the robust pale pink rose often used for hedging, has no English 'common name' because it was imported from Japan in the nineteenth century, although some people call it the Ramanas rose. However, this is no great advantage if you don't know that Ramanas is probably a corruption of the Japanese word for pear – and not that helpful, even then.

Some common names are just too common. 'Black Eyed Susan' is applied in different parts of the country to very different plants, all of which have a dark or black centre to their flower, but can be climbers or several different types of low growing plant. A plant with silver-spotted leaves and pink or blue flowers in spring has about a dozen different 'common names', from Lungwort to Spotted Dog to Soldiers and Sailors.

But Rudbeckia nitida (one sort of 'Black-Eyed Susan') is always the same plant, wherever in the world you are. Pulmonaria officinalis will always identify the same spotty plant growing under the tree.

Other names act as nicknames and are tagged on after. In the Ford Mondeo example, this is the model name, as in Ghia. The name of the variety or 'cultivar' is very important to the plant breeders and sellers, who market plants as 'Purple Wonder' or 'Cottage Delight'. But this name does not tell you if this is a rose, a lavender or an apple tree. If you just order a 'Purple Wonder', how do you know you will get the right plant?

The people who give plants their official names did not make life easy when they decided to name plants after botanists or explorers from Eastern Europe, like Paeonia mlokosewitschii, or decided to display their powers of Graeco-Latin description in a jawbreaker like Metasequoia glyptostroboides. But the system is useful, and no harder than memorising the names of new friends or colleagues (or cars).

You can pronounce these names any way you can – most people read or write them far more often than they try to say them. The peony is usually called 'Molly the witch' and everyone knows what you are talking about. The Metasequoia is referred to as 'That big tree over there.'

Modern botanists, incidentally, do not name their new discoveries immediately. Plants are given a bar-code depending on their DNA sequence, and when the botanists publish their discovery in an academic journal, the naming process starts.

DNA is also the reason why some old favourites have changed their official names, because some groups have been discovered to be very diverse and not to be a single 'family' after all. Chrysanthemums, as you buy in florists, are now botanically 'Dendranthemum' as a result.

The current problem is rosemary, which has been called that all over Europe for about two thousand years, but the botanist renamers have decided it's a 'salvia'. Occasionally, in a dark moment, one feels this is purely so someone can get an academic promotion.

Now go and read the rest of the book.

Planning in space and time

A return to First Principles

I collect old gardening books for several reasons: to remind me how fashion shapes what we want from our gardens, and to show how people coped before modern chemicals, powered equipment and - a hot topic now - plastic.

Here is how I set out principles for the new design of my latest garden, which is my Garden Five.

First, **manageability**, with a simple labour requirement and as few chemicals as possible. Warren Buffett, one of the world's leading business investors, said a company needs to be so simple that any idiot can run it, because one day, one will.

So if you need to loose your untrained nephew/kid/parent on your garden, Keep It Simple, Stupid (as the CIA say). This does not necessarily mean small, this is about approach, not acreage.

Second, **year-round use** and entertainment: warm sitting areas, a place for drying clothes, shady areas for when it gets hot, shelter from winter winds, a yard for necessary bins and sheds, and maybe an outdoor workspace for messier hobbies. Note this is not the 'room outside' kind of planning, because this kind of garden is not a room.

Third, **giving space to nature** and accepting passing wildlife, with somewhere to do its thing. Nature will anyway, especially in semi-rural areas like mine, so recognise this at an early stage in your design.

Now for the concerns of the twenty-first century. Let's **future-proof** by designing out the need for powered equipment other than battery or solar power, ditto the need for plastic as far as possible, and (for me) designing in hard surfaces, levels, steps and planting areas which I (and Igor my faithful servant) will be able to cope with for the next twenty years.

So, no long flights of steps or purely decorative changes of level, no slippery polished paving, broken concrete or uneven brick paviours, but gravel or bark mulch on paths and sitting areas. No fancy pruning needs, and as few hedges as possible.

However, I admit that - as of Garden Five - I've ended up with three big ones. There we go, best laid plans and all that. The birds like to nest in them, though.

Planning labour: Bang for your buck

There are three kinds of gardening that absorb a huge amount of labour and are unending: bare soil, tall hedges and bowling-green lawns.

Bare soil is an open invitation to weeds and even mulching is not a cure-all, close planting is more effective and more relaxed.

Hedges need clipping at least once a year, many twice or more. They take up a lot of space and water as well as casting dense shadow. Keep them if they're a feature but there are other ways to provide a screen or a windbreak, which do not involve dangling off a stepladder with a small chainsaw. If you 'get a man in', make sure they have a chainsaw certificate and insurance as chainsaws are very dangerous.

Lawns: in the old days, before mechanical lawnmowers, lawns were cut or scythed once a fortnight in the growing season, and they were not cut very close. If a dandelion offended your eye, you dug it out with a grubber.

Just allowing grass to get a little longer makes a big difference to the life in your garden. Fergus Garrett at Great Dixter has been overseeing a long-term study, with quite startling results.

Let the lawn get to two inches/five centimetres, and you double the amount of life it supports. Clover is one of the best bee plants. You'll never see cuckoo fowers or grassland orchids in your lawn if you cut it too close. Garrett's book on meadows, written with Christopher Lloyd, is well worth reading.

Your garden need not look like a patch of waste ground, unless you want the full hay-meadow effect, but most of us do not need a bowling green. If you do, in a small area, Astroturf is perfectly acceptable, although you will still need to weed. Thinking through your space, based on your budget, health and patience can save a lot of grief and family arguments.

Who's using the garden

Planning space in gardens feels difficult, because most people do not do it very often. 'Garden design' should not always mean lots of paving and expense, but should address who uses your garden, what for, and how much space they need.

There is no point in a fancy outdoor dining set if the patio is uncomfortably small, nor should parking space be so large that the local taxi company start making commercial enquiries about the front of your house.

Right, time to get out a big sheet of paper – or get up a spreadsheet, if you are happier on a computer.

Who will use the garden?

Put their names across in columns at the top. Now, what will they use it for?

To help you, here's a list of 18 suggestions:

1 Cricket pitch
2 Football pitch
3 Parties!
4 Hanging out the washing
5 Stage for the children's theatrical performances
6 Gymnasium
7 Swimming pool
8 Barbecue and entertainment space
9 Somewhere to park the caravan
10 A pond for the Koi carp
11 Dustbins (sorry - recycling bins)
12 Sundowners
13 Rumpus room (and part-time lavatory) for the dogs
14 Motorcycle strip-down area
15 Runs for the rabbits/guinea pigs/llamas/iguana
16 Reading room
17 Nude sun-bathing (surprisingly popular in a hot summer, as seen from high-speed trains)
18 Basketball court

You will note that some tarmac and a big piece of Astroturf can satisfy all of these requirements. Gardeners are not the only ones who use a garden.

Any plan that involves non-gardeners has to allow for this. Much cheaper than divorce. Every garden needs some open utility space. Even Vita Sackville West, the famous creator of Sissinghurst, used to eat in her garden and, for all I know, hung out her smalls as well.

When you put one space beside another, consider how they impact on each other; a greenhouse beside the basketball hoop is asking for tears. Smelly messy mechanical workspaces should be separate from quiet areas for sitting or sunning.

Areas for small children should be near the house for emergency medical/psychiatric/engineering help (as in "Mummy! The head's come off Teddy AGAIN and Chrissy's fallen over!"). Bigger children can survive a few metres of separation.

Assess how much space each activity takes and how many of them can comfortably share with each other. This will give a rough idea of the proportions you need to allow so that the garden is for everyone to enjoy.

What you want, what you need: priorities

Right. You've worked it out. There isn't enough room for everything.
Of course not, but don't panic.

Allow generous room, easily accessed, for things you and the household do regularly (like putting out dustbins, or using the hot-tub).
Don't assume paving is best. Grass is cheap, absorbs floodwater, is easy to patch, and kinder to children's knees.

The next rule is harder. Be generous with your chosen features.
Aim for patios, steps, ponds, or flowerbeds to be at least one metre across. Anything less looks fiddly and indecisive.
Very small gardens look best with a few big features, unless it's a mini-golf course.
Access paths should be at least 60 cm wide.

Simple shapes, like rectangles, triangles and circles, are not only better design but more practical, and simpler to do.
Big curves are much easier to mow round than squiggles.

A lesson from experience: work out the open space, first.

Say your garden is 6m by 10m, or 60 square metres (20 feet by 33, in old money). You think you want two-thirds as lawn. That's about 40 square metres, so say 4.5m by 9m.
But that means the borders around each side will be less than a metre wide, which will look mean and pinched. You will need to trim 27 metres of lawn edg You need a better balance.
Make the lawn slightly smaller, 8m by 4m (32 sq. m). Still usable, allows 1 metre on each side for trees and roses, and has 24 metres of edges.
A circular lawn 6 metres across - quick calculation - would be 28 square metres in area, look big and leave generous borders, and there are only 19 metres of edging.
But if you put a bed/pond/paving in the middle, 1 metre across, that adds another 3 metres of edging if circular, and 4 if square.
Keep it simple. Squiggles and beds cut out of a lawn can make an edge that is almost infinite.
Planning might need some arithmetic, but not rocket science. It's worth taking an hour now to save pain for the next twenty years.

The expensive bits: hard landscape

When looking at 'hard landscaping' such as paths and patios, you will probably have to buy your materials new but if you do have an architectural salvage yard nearby, go and have a look for bargains. But don't buy anything from some strange chap at the door, please.

Keep an eye out for ends of lines and sales at stone-merchants and builders' yards (they do have them). Bear in mind that the end to end cost may well be one third materials and two thirds labour.

You will spend something, but how much is up to you. A well-planned and executed garden should be useful and pleasurable for years. Don't begrudge some cost.

In a large and impressive house, a budget approaching that of a new kitchen or bathroom probably is not out of order. In a smaller house, compare your budget to the cost of a weekend away, or your latest electronic equipment.

Be careful with hard landscape like tarmac, paving and concrete. A large terrace or a concrete standing may seem an easy solution, but makes it very difficult to change your mind later.

Concrete is a particular problem, being both heavy and brittle, and so it requires deep footings. Over time, as the ground underneath shifts, the concrete may tilt or break. Slabs of concrete, no matter how carefully they were once laid, take a power hammer, a couple of men and a skip to remove.

There are alternatives. Under new legislation, front driveways for cars must now be made of material that allows rainwater to drain away, preventing flooding.

Materials that aren't concrete

Options include brick or stone paving laid on sand or a ballast foundation (a mix of rough gravel and broken brick) or gravel or other surface covering materials.

Don't dismiss grass, there are now mesh systems made of a very hard resin or metal in a honeycomb pattern, through which grass can grow and over which you can run a mower, but which give a tough surface for drives or hard standing.

For informal paths, the old way was to lay cinders from the open fire, which may still be an option in some places. The ash will tread into the earth with use, forming a dry, free-draining surface that only needs an occasional refresh and rake.

You can also use forest bark chippings in the same way. They will need topped up once in a while but are surprisingly effective: I use them in 'wild' bits. Bark can also be used in play areas but as it can be flammable when dry, not near the barbecue.

Gravel or shingle will need some sort of edging to stop stones spreading around, but is effective for paths, drives and seating areas. Don't lay fine gravel on a slope, however, as rain will wash it down.

In larger areas - wide paths or seating areas - cover the (cleared and vegetation-free) soil with landscape fabric first before putting down gravel or bark as this helps to prevent weeds coming though from beneath and any that do seed in are easily removed or raked out. Don't use plastic sheet as you need a material that will allow the rain to pass through.

The traditional material for laid paths is hoggin, a mix of gravel and heavy clay, but this will take a specialist with a machine, as hoggin needs to be pounded into place. Once down, hoggin is a firm surface.

Bricks, blocs, setts, paving slabs and stone are high cost options and all are best laid professionally. (If that's you, good on you, but otherwise hire that man again).

Paving will create a handsome setting for your house or seating area, as long as this is in proportion. You are embellishing the house and creating a practical usable area, not trying to recreate Horse Guards Parade. A house surrounded by huge amounts of bare paving looks bleak and can create a flooding problem.

How far down the garden you take expensive materials will depend on your pocket, and how formal an effect you want.

Bricks are less formal than paving or setts, but may flake in frosty weather. Any small paviour, like a brick or block, has to be set on a firm foundation or all sorts of humps and bobbles will appear after the frost has got into the soil underneath, and this can become a trip hazard.

In most professionally designed gardens, the hard landscape is by far the most expensive element, so like any permanent structure, think it through first.

Light, heat, and aspect

Using light across time

Winter can be a useful time to assess light in the garden. The low angle of winter sun can bring magical effects of silhouette, sun and shadow, and reminds us how important quality of light can be.

You can design this into your garden experience, from the tint of light itself to contrasts and angles. Low, weak winter sun picks out yellows and reds, as in holly berries and mahonia flowers, and golden conifers will glow against duller neighbours.

Winter rain washes dust out of the atmosphere, so light in spring is clear and 'cool'. This favours blue, greeny-yellow, and pinks with blue in them, like old-fashioned flowering cherries. However, warmer pinks can look muddy, especially under a grey shy.

Over summer, as the sun rises higher, light gets brighter and whiter but 'flattens' subtle colours. Bold colours and whites stand out strongly, as do big contrasts between light and shade.

Autumn light is warm: atmospheric dust has built up and the angle of the sun is low making the light yellower, an advantage to magenta, red, yellow and orange.

If your garden looks 'dull' at certain times of the year, use this colour effect to make it zing. However, some colours, like the greeny-pink of hellebores, will never be bright. These, and dark flowers like 'Queen of the Night' tulips or the darker dahlias, need to be close to the observer to be appreciated. At a distance, they fade out.

Contrast against background is also key. Plant dusky red Clematis 'Niobe' over a white wall, not against a dark fence. Red climbing roses are very popular, but can get lost against a red brick wall, while pale pink or yellow makes a better show. White climbers like jasmines or white potato vine look good against brick or wood, but may not be the most cheerful choice against flint. Try putting a book of paint colours against your wall or fence to see what works for you.

Using contrast and light together can transform impact. Light sings, but dark 'grounds' a scheme.

Golden-leaved plants need sun to turn a good colour, but not enough to scorch. They gleam even brighter against a dark or shady background.

Silver-leaved plants won't appreciate any sort of shade, but you can contrast them with dark evergreens like bay, palms or pines.

Purple leaves, like heucheras, need sun but benefit from 'lifting' by pale green or silvery neighbours.

Now the tricky stuff: backlighting. Some plants look tremendous when the sun shines through them. For this, the leaves or petals need to be thin. Young photinia leaves look scarlet, maples can be yellow through green to red, purple cotinus looks like rubies, and the golden catalpa will be a sunburst.

The plant has to be between you and the sun, and this is most marked when the sun is strong but low, in morning or late afternoon from mid-spring to autumn.

To get this effect, make up a 'plant' by tying a hula hoop to a six-foot cane, and cover the hoop with transparent coloured plastic or thin fabric. Now position your 'plant' as the sun goes across the sky, to see where best to put the real thing. Don't care what the neighbours think. Everyone will be deeply envious when they see your 'special effect'.

Managing heat

These days, we want the outside lifestyle to extend well into October, so how to maintain heat in a garden? 'Heat' can mean air temperature, which is how plants judge when to go into leaf or flower, or soil temperature, which lags air temperature by a few weeks as soil is a good insulator. Seeds and roots react to soil temperature so even if the air is warm, plants may not sprout until the soil catches up. But the barbecue chef will be most concerned with air temperature.

Heat is retained in dense, solid structures like timber, but most effectively in stone, tile, concrete or brick, which act as storage heaters. Slabs, blocks, gravel or chippings all heat up under direct sun. They then radiate heat and can raise the air temperature by a few degrees - the 'heat sink' effect.

But structures insulate both ways. Once cold, they retain a low temperature even if the day is warm. Think of chilly churches or cellars. A patio in a shaded, damp spot will remain cool and damp, which is great for moss and green stains. Not you, unless you're a frog.

The heat density of air is less than solids - you can put your hand in an oven at 200C, but not pick up a hot pan at that temperature. This is why warm air is not enough, on its own, to heat up soil or structures. You need direct energy and that means sun.

Noonday sun is 'hottest' because energy has travelled the least distance from the sun, so not lost much strength on the way. Sun from south or west is stronger than north or east.

For a hot patio, make it south-facing, paved or gravelled, and open to the sun from 11 a.m. to 3 p.m. To avoid heat - do the opposite.

Hot air is drier. This is good for a lot of Mediterranean plants, which may rot or get mildew otherwise. Also better for wooden furniture, but you might find it too baking to sit out without shade. Metal gets very hot very fast, so don't scald yourself on the patio set.

Hot gardens need shaded retreats as well. To create a steamy atmosphere - which some tropical plants adore - include a pond or fountain, for evaporation. Plants also create humidity because they transpire excess water through their leaves.

A hot patio with tubs of big leafy green plants, kept well-watered, will be locally humid and feel more 'buoyant' and comfortable, although not the full subtropical fug of a Caribbean or Florida garden. Gardens or patios with a lot of big leafy plants will be cooled by both shade and transpiration. Flowers on their own won't achieve this.

Soil temperature depends on direct exposure to sun. If soil is covered in leaves, dead or alive, it cannot heat up as much as when bare. So, give your tropical bedding a hand, sweep and weed the border, and let the soil get warm first.

White or pale surfaces reflect more heat than black. White absorbs least heat, which is why white marble stays feeling cool. But the reflected heat can raise air temperatures.

Black absorbs most heat. Black stone or timber may feel warm, but won't heat the air.

A hot patio is probably going to be a pale one. But don't forget the shading (and your sunglasses).

Unavoidable practicalities

Soil

Which plants do well will depend on what kind of soil you are trying to grow them in. What is soil for? Plants can and do survive without. Some are parasites on other plants, like mistletoe. Some, like many orchids, live on branches or sheer rocks, their roots holding fast but not feeding the plant.

Soil is, first and foremost, an anchor, so a plant stays upright and can point to the light.

Secondly, for many (but not all) plants, soil is where they get water.

Thirdly, water in soil contains trace elements. These are to plants what vitamins are to humans, not needed in huge quantity, but a problem when they are lacking.

Soil is made out of ground up rock, ground up dead plants, and ground up dead animals. Oh, yes - and dung. The rock is ground up by wind and weather.

Without the dead plants and animals, 'soil' is sand or gravel. 'Humus' is the polite name for the dead things that hold water and supply trace elements. Fungi and bacteria de compose the dead things. Earthworms finish the task by passing soil through their guts. And if that does not persuade you to get your tetanus jabs up to speed before you lift a garden trowel, I do not know what will.

Soil, especially 'good' soil, is alive with microorganisms, and some of these can cause problems if they end up in your bloodstream. Always wash your hands after gardening.

The active soil layer is normally not very deep The soil that plants grow in is typically from six inches/15 cm to two feet/60cm. Top-soil is the fertile layer at the (guess) top, which will be darker in colour and softer in texture than what lies beneath. Top-soil is where the plants put most of their roots, so this is where you need to concentrate as very few garden plants other than trees put down roots more than 3 feet/1 metre.

If roots meet a poor sub-soil layer or rock, they will tend to spread sideways, not down, because Nature isn't stupid. However, some plants need a minimum depth of soil to do well, so be aware that 'deep-rooted' plants may not adapt.

Even the largest trees do not get their roots down more than a few feet/metres, although they will root across by several metres. There were many visible demonstrations after the hurricane of 1987, which showed how shallow were the roots of many very big old trees.

The good news is you do not need to have lots of deep soil to grow a pleasant garden. The bad news is, it is still worth digging a hole about 60 cm deep or so in your patch, to show how much top-soil you have, whether the soil changes character as you go down, and probably where the water-table is, assuming you are not digging in a drought or live in a marsh or on a sand-dune.

Acid and alkaline soils

Take note, because I am about to save you a great deal of money.

One very important factor in your soil directly affects the kinds of plants you can grow. Is your soil acid or limy, and by how much?

Go down to your local garden centre or shop. Buy their simplest, cheapest pH test. pH is how chemists measure acidity or alkalinity, by the level of limestone or chalk in the soil.

Follow the instructions and take a reading of your soil. And take a look at your neighbours' gardens at the same time.

If acidity is 5 or less, you can easily grow rhododendrons, gentians, summer heathers, camellias, magnolias and other acid-lovers, and a camellia's leaves will be a deep dark burnished green.

However, if there are no rhododendrons in your neighbourhood, this means that chances are the soil isn't acid. This is because rhodies sell on sight at garden centres when they are in flower in May, and the only reason there aren't any is that they have all died. Which they will, expensively, on limy soil.

If acidity is 7 or upward, you can't grow acid-lovers, at least not directly in the soil. But you can grow them in tubs, like I do. You can easily grow thyme, rosemary and other herbs, buddleias, pinks and the vast majority of other plants.

If acidity is around 6 to 7, or neutral, you can grow camellias etc. but their leaves may turn yellowish and you might need to give them special feed like sequestered iron or Epsom salts.

One other clue is the colour of your neighbours' hydrangeas. If they are all blue, it's acid. If they are all pink, it's alkaline. If they are muddily lilac, it's in between. If they are all white, you're in a hotbed of garden fashion and upmarket shrub-fanciers, so your neighbours will tell you (or their gardeners).

Acid soils are usually found in areas with lots of peat, but some types of underlying rock are acid and even thin grainy soils can be acid. The ground-up granites of Cornwall, Cumbria or the Highlands give an acid soil, as do the greensands found in parts of the Midlands and South East.

If there is a lot of rainfall, any natural lime in the soil may be washed out, because limestone is soluble, so acid soils are more common in the wet West than the dry East.

River-mud can contain a lot of ground up limestone and dissolved chalk, as rivers carve their way through these soft rocks and carry them away. So if you are near a river your soil is more likely to be limy (alkaline).

As most cities are built on river plains, that covers a lot of the urban areas of the UK, including most of South-East England. If you live on the Downs, the Wolds, the Cotswolds or any of the other great limestone hill systems, your soil is probably alkaline. But test all the same, as you may be on a pocket of acid soil or greensand.

You can increase acidity in soils by adding more organic materials such as dead leaves, manure and com post, and you can add ground up limestone to acid soils, but you cannot change underlying geology. Unless you import all your topsoil (and I know gardeners who have done this) you have what the geology gives you. And even if you do import your topsoil, after some years – yep, the geology pokes through again.

Soil improvement, and upsetting the neighbours

The organic argument is that you will only need to use remedies for your plants if the basic health of your garden falters and that with a healthy soil, this should not happen. The usual recommendation is to add plenty of good garden compost and well-rotted manure to the soil.

Which only goes to prove that most of the people who write this kind of thing have never gardened in an urban terraced house with no rear access.

Garden compost, no matter how good, may condition the soil but does nothing for carpet. And for manure to get to the stage of being well-rotted, it has to start out fresh, which is how stables (and horses) supply it. And you have to get said manure from the stable to your front door, which means using the car...

Of course, if you do have a rear access, and you can take bulk deliveries without setting the entire neighbourhood against you, stable manure or poultry litter is an excellent soil conditioner. You will need a surprisingly large amount even for an average garden, however, and there will be a pong. For a long time.

The compost question

Compost is also more of a vexed question than many writers admit. Compost is what happens to vegetable matter, whether leaves, stems, roots or other bits and pieces, when it undergoes a controlled partial fermentation.

Making compost is not just a matter of dumping a load of prunings in a heap and hoping for the best. Compost needs moisture, to encourage the fungi and bacteria to break the vegetation down, and heat, to keep everything ticking over.

The heap needs to be netted or otherwise shielded to stop rats and mice from nesting. Ideally the whole lot needs to be turned, from top to bottom, every couple of months.

Vegetation will create heat as it begins to rot. One garden writer has mentioned his surprise, on making a very large mixed salad, to find how warm it had become after a couple of hours. But the heat will not be retained unless the heap is large enough, or well insulated.

The minimum size for a non-insulated heap is a metre square. Heat will only start to be generated in a heap a couple of feet/60 cm high. A domestic heap will never achieve the very high temperatures of the large heaps operated by parks departments and commercial composters, which effectively sterilise the compost.

So, your heap will always contain weed seeds and will never fully break down woody material. Some leaves take a very long time to break down, notably oak leaves, because they contain high levels of tannin, which is the stuff used to preserve leather.

You can insulate your bin, or buy a ready-insulated one. Insulation in this case means a polystyrene wall about two inches/5 cm thick all round, with a lid to match.

It goes without saying that most of the green plastic bucket-like constructions sold as compost bins are simply too small when un-insulated to create the proper conditions for controlled composting.

You still need to produce enough material to build the heap up relatively quickly. You might club together with some neighbours and make a 'street heap' (remembering the potential rat problem). In the old days, you could burn dry rubbish and spread the resulting potash, but local authorities discourage this now because of smoke pollution.

If you do construct a heap, although in theory a finished compost heap might be ready to use in two months, in practice allow six or more. In a cold season, or for a heap with a lot of twigs, it is sensible to leave the heap for a year.

Alternatives to the compost bin

A shredder might bypass the problem altogether. These cost about as much as a lawn-mower, will take green stuff, twigs and branches up to an inch/2 cm across, and the chippings they produce can be spread on the garden immediately. But don't try shredding phormium (New Zealand Flax) leaves – they twist round and round the blade and will not break.

In ornamental plantings, spread compost, shredding etc on top as mulch, in a layer up to 4 inches/10 cm thick. If you do this at the end of autumn, the worms will pull it down. If you do dig in, do so lightly. Shreddings, as noted above, can be spread without waiting for additional fermentation and will degrade naturally over the winter.

There are other 'organic' alternatives. Treated poultry manure and other concentrated natural manures are available commercially, although this will not add bulk to the soil. However, straw or lawn clippings will, especially if you spread them in autumn and let the worms drag them down.

Conditioning your soil is possible, but is not a short-term process, can be expensive, and is not a cure-all. You will still get pests, although one hopes your plants will look healthier most of the time, and it should gradually become possible to dig without either a pick-axe or a dust-mask.

Weeds

Round about June, with a sufficient amount of sun and rain, your garden should be burgeoning with growth. However, round about now, a lot of people start to feel completely overwhelmed and start muttering about concrete or decking, because the growth the garden is burgeoning with, is weeds. What to do? First of all, very few weeds are life-threatening (or even home-threatening).

There are four you really need to know about, because it is now illegal to plant them or spread them, you can't even throw them over your fence, and you can be fined or imprisoned if you do.

However, you can put most in your green waste bin, because council tips compost at a temperature high enough to kill them and their seeds.

The illegal four are
Japanese knotweed (Fallopia japonica)
Giant hogweed (Heracleum mantegazzianum)
Himalayan balsam or policeman's helmets (Impatiens glandulifera)
The common purple rhododendron (ponticum).

Knotweed can devalue your house because it is so persistent, and needs to be controlled with special chemicals by an approved operator. (This might take several seasons).

Giant hogweed produces blistering stems and is easily spotted as it is two to three metres high, and the balsam also grows to two metres. (You should not compost these or put them in green waste. Poison these and bag the remains - see the council website for disposal).

Rhododendron ponticum, the wild purple rhodendron, is a smotherer and poisonous to cattle. If you have ragwort in your garden and you're near farmland, this should be removed for the same reason.

There are other plants which are **illegal to spread, sell, exchange or put in the wild** under EU/UK rules. If they already in your garden you do not need to take them out, but be aware you can't give them away.

A lot are exotic/aquarium waterweeds, so the first rule there is, get them out of your outdoor pond (including the old aquarium favourite, Canadian pondweed). The list also includes American skunk cabbage, Lysichiton americanus, which has yellow flowers. See the DEFRA website for up to date information.

Other plants defined as '**invasive**' in the UK are:
Hottentot fig (Caprobotus edulis)
Some cotoneasters: bullatus, horizontalis, integrifolius, microphyllus, simonsii

Allium triquetrum (three-leaved ransoms)
Montbretia (Crocosmia crocosmiflora)
Gunnera tinctoria (but not manicata)
Yellow archangel/yellow dead nettle (Lamiastrum galeobdolon)
Virginia creeper (Parthenocissus quinquefolia or inserta)
Yellow azalea (Rhododendron luteum) (wild species, not named garden varieties)
Rosa rugosa (wild species, not named garden varieties)

You can continue to grow these if they are already in your garden but you should not be able to buy them from reputable suppliers without a warning label. But check your church bazaar purchase or Granny's gift.

Ideally, don't choose to grow these, and if you want to get rid of them from your land, follow council guidelines for disposal. The RHS, Plantlife and DEFRA websites keep up to speed on these.

A small number of wild plants are actively **poisonous** but most are not usually found in gardens. As I'm sure you tell your children, check with an expert before eating anything from the garden even if it's 'wild'.

I thought long and hard about including a list of the most poisonous garden plants but you know what? If you want to murder your partner, do the search on your own computer, not mine.

Other 'weeds' might be inconvenient but aren't likely to do you an injury. Some are simply wild flowers with the temerity to grow in lawns, like daisies and most hawkweeds, which are like wispy dandelions. Ditto buttercups, and even moon-daisies. I just let them get on. Not every lawn needs to be a bowling green.

Persistent perennial weeds include ground elder, horsetail, creeping buttercup and dandelions, and the big white bindweed (convolvulus). These send out roots that can create new plants if the top growth is removed, so you have to dig out or kill the whole plant.

Digging out is rarely practical, although on a damp soil, you can get dandelion roots out with a daisy-grubber. At this point, currently I do reach for the glyphosate to spray on growing leaves, but may need a replacement if glyphosate is banned.

Spare a thought for the horsetail, a primitive plant survivor for over 400 million years - at least some of you drew them at school when you were taught about how coal was formed. They are also called 'scouring rush' because they have high levels of silica, to stop dinosaurs eating them, and so were used to polish metal. But a nuisance, all the same.

A dose in May or June should get on top of most of these although they might need another dose in September. Don't cut your weeds back first: the larger the surface area the weedkiller can access, the better.

Now the case for leaving some weeds alone. You might not appreciate a lot of nettles, but Red Admirals and other butterflies will appreciate having some for their caterpillars to eat. Elder bushes and brambles are good wildlife habitats, so be selective, and leave some grasses to get long, again for the caterpillars of butterflies and pollinators. Most of the other stuff is annual and shallow-rooted and can be hoed out but unless you're very keen on hoeing, remember that the best way to prevent weeds is to grow something else.

Nature abhors a vacuum. Bare ground has to be the most labour-intensive form of gardening there is. So take out the weed and put something else in. And relax.

Poisons

While clearing out an old garage and greenhouse, I found enough stuff to do away with half my neighbourhood. And there is a real possibility that glyphosate, 'Round Up', may be banned because it is deemed to be potentially cancer-causing.

When I began serious gardening in the 1970's, every 'popular gardening' book would include a large chapter on killing things like wasps, flies, worms, ants, greenfly, whitefly and blackfly, moths, mice, and moles.

And there were fungicides and chemicals to sterilise, fertilise, acidify, break up or disinfect soil. And creosote derivatives to smoke, wash down or paint greenhouses and sheds.

And DDT, lindane, permethrin, diquat and paraquat. Herbicides 2,4,5-T and 2,4-D were still in garden use until 1985 which, mixed together, make Agent Orange.

Like everyone else in that generation I took chemicals very seriously, stocked up on goodies like malathion and sulphur, and I sprayed my roses and fruit religiously. Until I realized that the main thing being sprayed for pests was me. And I did notice that paraquat was not only highly toxic to humans but had no antidote.

Since then, especially since the 2004 international ban on the so-called 'dirty dozen', which are not only dangerous but 'persistent' in natural systems, the number of chemicals that gardeners can use legally has dropped sharply.

Permitted chemicals or physical barriers

Very few garden pesticides are now legally permitted, and in 2019, blue slug pellets were also banned (metaldehyde). Organic gardeners have almost no permitted pesticides. A dispensation exists for Bordeaux mixture, a copper sulphate mix for use on grapes, and for derivatives of soft soap.

This is not because of prejudice against gardeners. Most garden chemicals are made by companies whose primary business is agriculture. Controls are guided by impacts on farm workers as well as the broader agricultural system. (And you, if you're within the spray drift of a farm).

Any 'agrichemical' has to be tested and approved separately for a specific use, and this costs money. This may be worthwhile for products sold to farmers, but the scale of the home gardening market is much smaller, so it may not make financial sense. The number of agrichemical companies has fallen rapidly and not all choose to maintain products in home gardening.

So what's left? Physical barriers - netting, grease bands, copper strips, and wool pellets - do no harm and can be safely left out in family gardens. Squishing works, too.

Biological controls such as pheromone traps, nematodes and parasitic wasps are used in enclosed spaces. Kew Gardens, Wisley and most commercial glasshouse growers use these, because they are highly efficient.

Some 'organic' sprays are available, notably rotenones and pyrethrins, insecticides obtained from plants and dissolved in detergent. But, like any contact insecticide, they will kill any creature they land on, including bees, so use carefully.

Some 'pests' are just an annoyance. Blue tits, ladybirds and hoverflies will have most aphids. Earwigs nibble things but do not kill them. Ants, unless they invade your kitchen, are just part of the garden. And no gardener who wants to go to Heaven should ever kill an earthworm.

Treat any chemicals with care, make sure they are correctly labelled, never leave them where children or pets can get to them and use as sparingly as you can.

And when, like me, you have to dispose of old nasties, take them to the hazmat section of a waste depot. Never, ever just pour them away down a drain.

Making more

When faced with an empty new garden, don't immediately assume a huge bill for buying plants. If you are moving from an old garden or you have friends and rellies with a garden, you can make loads without much expense. Propagation is a topic in its own right. If you do get interested, seek out a reliable book, such as the RHS Handbook.

Note: A lot of gardening books show grafting, but as no normal hobby gardener EVER does this, don't worry about it.

Division

This is the easy way, and you won't kill most garden plants by dividing them. Say you have a large clump of daylilies, marguerites, hardy geraniums or hostas, which is so magnificent you'd like a few more. Get your digging fork under the clump, loosen it, and heave it out of the ground. Lots of roots will wave at you.

Split the clump into a few big pieces, using a hand-fork and brute strength, or you can saw it apart: I use an old kitchen knife. Put a chunk back, take the other chunks to their new holes, and plant them. Keep them watered, if you're doing this in spring or summer. Don't be tempted to cut the clump into too many small pieces as plants need to be big enough to grow away well.

Many herbaceous plants split but not all. Some, such as oriental poppies, have a tap-root, which looks like a pale carrot. Apologise to the plant and put it back.

Some popular plants, like wallflowers, penstemons and pinks, have a woody base, so take cuttings (see below).

Spring bulbs can be divided after flowering as some, like daffodils, stop blooming if they're overcrowded. Lift and split as above. You should be able to pull the bulbs apart with your hands. You can make 'Incredible Hulk' noises if you like.

Cuttings

You can fool a plant into producing roots from within a stem or branch, in response to injury. Roots are formed by hormones that are at their densest just under the 'skin' of the plant.

In early summer, cut off a small, bendy branch of a shrub like fuchsia, lavender or hebe, or shoots of plants like pinks. These should be about 10-15 cm long. Rub off any little side shoots and all leaves from the bottom 5 cm. Dip the bottom in some water, then into some fresh (this year's!) hormone rooting powder.

Place 4 or so cuttings along the edge of a 6-8 cm pot of compost, burying the bottom half. Put your pot on a tray, water it, and cover with a plastic dome.

Leave the tray somewhere outside that's cool but not cold, and shaded. If water droplets form inside the cover, shake them out. Put the cover back. After two weeks or so, if the leaves look and feel stiff, take the cover off. Some cuttings will die, but don't worry about that.

Get rid of dead leaves and stems. If the pot feels light and leaves look wilted, water and put the cover back for another couple of days. In a few weeks, roots should start coming out of the bottom of the pot.

Congratulations! You are the proud parent of a cutting.

For shrubs, when you see new leaves AND roots, move each into their own, larger, pot, but wait until next spring to plant them out. Herbaceous plants can go out in autumn.

Some plants root at the drop of a hat, like pinks and wallflowers. Fuchsias, some pinks and winter jasmine will root in a glass of water. But some are distinctly iffy.

'Root cuttings' are useful for some plants with thick roots, like the oriental poppies or eryngiums, and also phlox. Lift the plant, cut off a couple of the roots, remember which end is the top, and cut the roots into 5-6 cm lengths. Set them out, top to the top, in a pot like the shrub cuttings we did before.

Not used as often but handy for some plants.

Seeds

These can be difficult, so start with easy ones, by which we mean big ones. Little seeds are very light and often very hard to get going, as they don't have much food within the seed for the plant embryo.

Nasturtiums, runner beans and marigolds (calendula or tagetes) are all easy to sow. In April or May, fill a small pot with some growing medium ('potting compost') and firm it down with your knuckles, but not hard. Water it. Place your seeds into the pot – about half a dozen per pot. Cover them either with a little more compost, or a layer of vermiculite (explained below). Water again. Place on a seed tray.

Put somewhere relatively warm but not hot – the shaded side of a sunny greenhouse, or a windowsill in a cool bedroom. Keep watered, but not so much that the tray becomes heavy, and take any mildewed or rotten leaves away. Make sure the seedlings have enough light and do not get too hot or they will be pale and drawn. If they have several leaves and start getting tall, nip the top of the shoot out with your fingers.

As the plants bush out, be ready to separate them and put each into a pot, or the final growing position in the garden. Keep watered. Seeds grow best in a medium that is light but not very fertile. The whole point of a seed is that it has its own food supply. They are also sensitive to rots and mildew. Many need light to germinate so check your seed packet.

I now mix a seed compost that is half commercial growing medium and half vermiculite, or you could use perlite. Both are types of rock which have been exploded under pressure into lightweight granules used to increase drainage. If you use either to top off pots of seeds or cuttings, they let light through, and also discourage algae and weeds from growing on the surface.

Plants that sow themselves

You may not need to mess around with seed packets, if you have the conditions for plants to seed themselves.

If you have forget-me-nots, for example, one plant will produce quite enough seedlings to keep you, and the whole county, stocked up for next spring. However, the plants will not necessarily look the same as their parents.

If you have highly bred columbines (aquilegia), for example, their seedlings will not be in the bright colours and combinations of the bought-in flowers. They will 'revert' to their natural colours and shapes, in this case a range of white, pink, lavender and maroon, without the long spurs behind the flower.

If you are happy with the natural shades, then reliable self seeding annual or perennial flowers include forget-me-nots, aquilegia, nigella (love in a mist), ox-eye daisies, pulmonaria, Crocus tommasinianus, honesty, foxgloves, small violas and cowslips.

In damp conditions, primroses and hellebores will spread. In hot dry places, California poppy, peony-flowered ('opium') poppy, poached-egg plant (limnanthes), alyssum and calendula will grow for you.

Some shrubs also spread by seed. Many seeds love being in gravel. In my gravel driveway in Garden Three I had woolly lavender (Lavandula lanata), sea holly (Eryngium planum), the little yellow Achillea ageratum, thyme and a couple of hebes, all of which came there by themselves.

When one of my bamboos flowered a few years ago (Fargesia murielae), a small forest of seedlings came up in the cracks between the paving on the terrace where the tub had been standing. So it's always worth teaching yourself to recognise seedlings and if you want to let Nature do some of the work, let some of your plants find their own place in your garden.

Seeders for Big Effects

Some of the most striking seasonal plant effects are drifts and vistas such as woodland swathes of bluebells or white anemones, a shingle beach covered in horned poppy, vipers' bugloss and seakale, or a meadow of cowslips or moon daisies. Now a rare sight, there used to be fields of poppies, cornflowers and other open farmland flowers.

What these have in common, is that all of them arrive by seed, in their many thousands. Plants can be extraordinarily prolific with their seed, which is to our advantage, so we don't have to buy hundreds of little plants and then dig holes for them. We can let mature plants spread their seed for us.

In the UK, seed is normally set from June onwards, so the little plants can grow during the autumn and be big and fat for next season's flowers. Our mild, wet winters mean that only those whose germination is triggered by frost will wait until spring. As long as we don't hoe them out in our September clearout, that is. Exotics needing a dry winter and a wet spring won't do so well.

So, if you don't already have a parent plant spraying seed about, September is the time to open-sow old favourites in some clear ground for big effects: forget-me-nots, corn marigolds, cornflowers, nigella, peony-flowered poppies.

In shady places, go for foxgloves, honesty, and nettle-leaved bellflowers (Campanula trachelium). In dry areas, try California poppy, Anthemis cupaniana, and the silver sea-holly (Eryngium giganteum) called Miss Wilmott's Ghost. Now learn to recognise their babies so you don't weed them out. Next year, remember to let them seed themselves.

These are annual or biennial, so you may get two or three years out of each plant.

But some fast-growing perennials will fill in spaces or create massed effects (or for potting up for plant fairs, or gifts).

Spring flowers: Primroses and cowslips should be the Sussex county flowers; they are generous in their seeding almost to a fault.

Lady's mantle (Alchemilla mollis) likes steps, border edges, and gravel.

In light, warm shade hellebores, especially Corsican hellebore, (Helleborus argutifolius) will create metre-high clumps.

Columbines (Aquilegia) like sun or shade. Welsh poppies (Meconopsis cambrica) like a little shade.

Summer plants: in a hot, gravel drive, lavender will seed happily.

Goat's rue (Galega officinalis) is bushy, 2 metres high, lilac or white.

Musk-mallow (Malva alcea) gets to 60 cm/2 feet and has parsley-like leaves and clean pink or white flowers.

Several border bellflowers seed about, notably Campanula persicifolia, latifolia, and nettle-leaved bellflower (Campanula trachelium).

A special word for Sisyrinchium striatum: look it up – you'll know it when you see it.

Autumn flowers: Michaelmas dairies seed EVERYWHERE, but the genetic tombola creates some that are tough, mildew-resistant and attractive: weed the losers and keep the winners.

The small autumn cyclamen will seed freely in half-shade.

Some of the bigger stuff that will turn up given half a chance includes Aaron's rod (Verbascum thapsus) which has 2 metre silver spires of yellow flowers, Scotch thistle (Onopordium, also 6 foot/2 metres) and, in hot spots, the shrubby spurge (Euphorbia characias, 3 foot/1 metre).

Any plant that sets seed CAN have babies, of course, and depending on your local conditions, you might get a patch of hollyhocks, Portugal laurel, or cordylines (cabbage palm). But none of this will happen if you insist on hoeing everything away between your plants, or have a heavy hand with mulch. Learn to leave things alone until you can see what they are.

Bluebells, incidentally, are best left for the woods. They spread like wildfire but – as I'm sure many know – it's an offence to dig them up. Lots of good reasons for this, but it makes them bad neighbours in a garden.

Allergies

Most of us have some sort of allergy – very few escape a bout or three of hay fever in June, and for some, high summer just means red eyes and streaming noses. A lot of us have contact allergies, too. It does not take much to get sensitised to touching hyacinth bulbs, or rue, and the mixture of conifer sap and sunlight can not only blister but leave brown tattoo marks behind. (Been there, done that).

For most of us, allergies are a passing nuisance but for those with strong reactions, they can be a really limiting condition. But this does not mean you're banned from the garden.

Pollen: You can be allergic to almost anything but most 'hay fever' is caused by air-borne pollen. The sticky bright yellow pollen you see on flower stamens like lilies is obvious, but not a main cause of allergy, not least because most of us do not spend our lives surrounded by lilies.

The main plants that release dusty pollen into the air and cause allergies are grasses, whether wild, lawn or ornamental, and trees like willow, hazel, alder, poplar, ash, beech and birch, which are all catkin-flowerers. Another high-summer culprit is oil-seed rape.

'Fluff' can be a problem for some people. Some trees and plants are generous with their seedheads, notably willows, reeds, bulrushes, willow-herb, goldenrod and plane trees. In some seasons, river-banks can seem covered in willow 'snow'.

Note that conifers such as pines, although they do not have flowers, release a lot of pollen into the wind, this being the male sex cell in plants. Yews shed so much it can look like clouds of smoke in April and May, and both cypresses and junipers can cause pollen allergy or contact dermatitis.

Flowers: Most flowers we grow in gardens for decoration do not release pollen into the wind. You might wish to avoid the daisy and sunflower types as they have flat, open flowers where pollen can blow off, and in some, fluffy seeds.

Flowers that attract bees try to keep their pollen on the stamen and do not usually cause a pollen reaction, so bedding, fruit trees, grapevines, roses and most herbaceous plants should be fine.

Another way to avoid pollen is to grow double or sterile flowers. In most plants, 'doubling' is created when pollen structures are transformed into small extra petals. Conversely, if you want to attract bees and insects, single flowers attract many more than doubles. A highly doubled rose - no matter how strong the scent – is not going to produce much, if any, pollen.

Scents can make you sneeze, but not many actually react with your lungs or skin. Even though flowers releasing cyanides such as oleanders and the cherry (Prunus) family are theoretically poisonous, this is not in sufficient quantity, in an open space, to be a problem.

Many people find linden (Tilia or 'lime') overpowering. Other strong scents such as hawthorn, choisya leaves, Asiatic lilies or carnations have unpleasant connotations for some, but won't do you any physical harm. Even arums that absolutely reek, notably Arum sauromatum or the dranunculus types, are harmless.

Contact allergies are annoying. Some plants known to cause reactions are rue, chrysanthemums, lavender, the artemisia (wormwood) family and the bulbs of daffodil, tulip or hyacinth. However, dealing with these is easy. Wear gloves.

Allergies should always be taken seriously but unless you know you really have a specific chemical or asthmatic reaction, this is not a reason to avoid the garden. Recent research is showing that air-fresheners and polishes may be causing far more irritants inside our homes than any plant outside.

Gardening by season

Nature's timing, or lack of.

If you look around your neighbourhood in late August or early September, only too often this is a depressing sight. The year feels over already. So why are British gardens such a sad sight in the post-June collapse? Well, part of the reason is nature, and part commerce.

The good news is, neither is insurmountable. Britain is a northern European country with a damp climate. This means the natural growing season is from about February to June, after which most native plants try to set seed or go to fruit.

Many plants form their flowers for the next year in the summer, to be ready for the off when spring comes around again. Plants which leave flowering until later risk getting beaten by drought at their most sensitive time, in midsummer. They may also get frosted when their new fruits are about to be dropped in late autumn.

As a result, the showiest native flowers are spring or early summer ones, like snowdrops, primroses, bluebells, daffodils, violets, and wild roses. These are also on most people's must-have list, if only because most people can recognise what they are. They are the stuff of nursery rhymes and poetry. My love may be like a red, red rose, but never a dahlia as they had not become popular in Britain when Burns wrote his lines. So for a good show from July onwards, you need to do some planning.

Plants that flower later are usually imports, even if they are of long standing, like chrysanthemums. Many later flowerers come from countries where winters are dry, or so cold that growth is impossible. These plants have to grow and flower within the same season.

Although we may love our dahlias, red-hot pokers, chrysanthemums and Michaelmas daisies, they are all foreigners, less familiar and sometimes more demanding than the natives.

Commercial availability

The commercial aspect of plant availability is determined by school holidays. Garden centres and nurseries can sell any amount of spring shrubs and roses, because at Easter - or spring half-term, if Easter is late - these are either in flower, or have helpfully bright labels, meaning that Daddy can look as if he knows what he's buying. Easter Monday is usually the busiest day in garden centres in the UK.

But if a plant has no flowers or is an unfamiliar name, Daddy (or Mummy, ignorance isn't sexist) will tend to leave it alone. Unless the plant comes into flower or otherwise looks impressive over their next couple of visits, the centre will not sell it.

When the schools come out in July, the business rush is over, everybody goes on holiday and so plants with a July to September flowering season will not get much opportunity to impress potential buyers.

Garden centres will gladly stock all sorts of plants, but only if they can sell them. To break the cycle, look at the seasonal recommendations in this book, and seek out a centre that will supply or order them for you.

Plants do not flower against a calendar. Although most will flower in or near the period mentioned, if the season is unusually warm or cold, this will affect flowering dates. Gardens in the north/nearer the Pole/a long way from the sea have shorter summers than those in the south and west or on a coast.

The gardener's calendar

Gardeners have calendars, plants don't.

Your workload will be guided but not determined by the date. Plants respond to light, water and temperature.

If we have a late (cold) spring, in the UK the daffodils may not appear until April. In an early one, they will start flowering in February.

In the olden days of cottage gardening, you will be told that the cottagers would plant their potatoes at Easter. As the date of Easter moves about by seven weeks, because it is calculated by phases of the moon, this is not because 'Easter' is always a good time to plant things. But it was one of the few free days that agricultural workers had, to dig the veg patch and put in the potatoes.

However, there are some useful dates in the year where you can stop and take stock of what's happening. All dates refer to the UK. Australians will know to add six months and, in the USA, you will be guided by how far north you are.

New Year's Day/Hogmanay

Does your garden look well furnished with evergreens, berries and maybe the odd snowdrop, or is the scene bleak? Take a note for the spring planting season. Between now and end of March is the best time to prune grapevines, clematis and roses, because the plants will be dormant (not in growth).

Finish planting your big shrubs and trees, but don't plant ornamental grasses or the Mediterraneans yet (see April). If you need to do work on trees and large bushes, now is a good time. Be aware

it is now illegal in the UK to disturb nesting birds, and most contractors will not look at work on trees or hedges after March through to May.

Candlemas, about 2nd February

Near Chinese New Year, or, if you are a Celt, Imbolg, when the first lambs are born. The quality of daylight will be noticeably improved and temperatures will start to rise. In the UK we can still get snow until April, but this is when spring should start to feel nearer. New Yorkers are allowed a hollow laugh. We know it's still well below freezing over there.

Finish the clearing up, cut down dead heads on your herbaceous plants, trim up shrubs that flower from June onwards. If you cut back spring-flowering shrubs now, you are cutting off this year's flowers.

If the weather is warm enough, dig over the vegetable patch and clear off the weeds.

Spring Equinox, 21st March.

Daffodils and blossom should be around, also crocus and other little bulbs. If your garden looks bare compared to others, take a note for which bulbs to buy in August and September.

Glimpse your first butterfly. These are usually pale yellow (brimstone) or white and orange (orange tip), if you have plants of honesty or dame's rocket nearby.

Cut off dead bits of shrubs which did not come through the winter, these will be dry and brittle. But if you are in any doubt, leave until midsummer, to see if they sprout.

Finish pruning roses.

If you are going to dig a new bed or lay out garden structures, you can start marking them out now, but only progress them if the weather will not freeze again. In a warm year, start mowing.

St George's Day, 23rd April.

All the dandelions are in flower.

Now you can usually plant new plants of lavender, rosemary, cistus, sage, thyme, other grey-leaved plants, chrysanthemums, grasses, red-hot pokers, ornamental grasses and other plants that might rot off if you put them too soon into a cold wet soil. If still boggy, hold off another couple of weeks.

Shape old rosemary, lavender, cotton lavender, thyme etc. by cutting back by about a third. If they are terminally straggly, terminate them. Young plants grow fast.

Cut the dead flowers off winter-flowering heathers and trim the bushes to shape. Please. If a bunch of dead twigs is the result – replace them. Please.

It's still too soon for bedding, though, so leave the trays of marigolds at the garden centre, unless you have a greenhouse to put them in. You can begin to buy young tomato plants for the greenhouse.

Enjoy your daffs and early tulips, sow some nasturtiums in the greenhouse or on a windowsill, and work out if there are any clumps of plants which you want to divide or move. On a warm day, do that.

Start the big outside jobs like constructing greenhouses, sheds, patios or conservatories. April can bring a very cold snap, called the 'Blackthorn Winter' because it comes when the blackthorn (the fluffy white stuff that isn't hawthorn) is in flower, but if the soil is warm this should not put plants back too much.

Chelsea Flower Show week, about 21st May

Now you can put your bedding and tender plants outside. You still have time to sow some seeds as well; in warm damp conditions, they will sprout very fast.

Finish planting trees and shrubs and moving, splitting and replanting smaller plants. If you plant in dry hot conditions later, your plants may not be able to access enough water from the soil or create new roots. You will need to keep them watered through hotter months, which could be a major task.

Enjoy your first roses.

Don't tie the daffodil leaves in knots as they will die back naturally by June.

Cut your hedges, and prune spring-flowering shrubs as they finish, like forsythia (see Pruning).

Midsummer Day, 21st June/Wimbledon

A bit of a misnomer. Air takes a while to heat up in the first half of the year, so June can be quite cool. This is better regarded as the start of the English summer. So, does your garden look summery?

Take a note now, but the best time to buy roses, shrubs etc. is autumn. You still have time to buy bedding or tender plants to beef up the display, but think big, as they won't have so long to grow.

Your first vegetable crops will be ready, and if you have gooseberries and early strawberries, so will they. The clover will be flowering so leave the mowing for a couple of weeks.

Lammas/Lughnasa, 1st August

Ladymass, or the old Celtic festival of the 'First Harvest'. Has your garden survived past the end of June? A lot of gardens fall to pieces because not enough thought has been given to the August/September show, when the weather is often better than in June.

You should have roses, evergreens and grey-leaved plants, which often look at their best now, bedding, and plants from the Mediterranean and South Africa like red-hot pokers.

August Bank Holiday, 31st August

Like New Year's Day, a time to take note of what's working and what isn't. The first apple and pear crops will be coming in.

Strawberries can still be picked if you have planted so-called perpetual varieties. The vegetable patch should be in full fling.

The first daffodil bulbs will be in the garden centre and, astonishingly, this is the best time to buy and plant them. Daffies put their roots out very early. Tulips can wait until October or November.

Autumn Equinox, 21st September

Make a list of the new plants you want, and the existing plants that no longer do the job. If you've thought ahead, you should have a good show from all sorts of Michaelmas daisies, ice plant (sedum), perovskia (Russian sage), yellow daisies and sunflowers (rudbeckia, heliopsis, helianthus, coreopsis), echinacea, chrysanthemums, and tender plants like dahlias.

Roses will still be going strong.

We often get a warm period in the beginning of October called 'St Martin's Little Summer, so plan to enjoy your outdoor space until at least then.

If the sloes are ripe (dark blue and softish), pick them and fill a wide-mouthed jar (you can prick them with a needle to start the juice coming out). Pour sugar over them to half the depth of the jar, then pour gin over to cover right up to the top. Screw the lid down and leave until Christmas. Also do this with damsons or blackberries.

Halloween/All Souls/Samhain, 31st October

Pretty well the end of the gardening year, so plant the remaining spring bulbs, compost the summer bedding, cut off the last roses (they'll just rot in the winter), rake up the leaves, and clear areas where you are going to put new plants or borders. Probably, stop mowing.

Then go to the garden centre or nursery and spend a lot of money on trees and bushes. That's the fun bit. Then come home and plant them all. Which may not be so much fun. But, as noted above, leave the grey-leaved and tender plants until the spring.

If you want and you have a few tubs in sheltered places to fill, then winter flowering pansies, primulas and heathers can give a show, and the little cyclamens are pretty but not that tough. Plant your tulips and wallflowers.

Sensibly, that's the last sustained work of the season because the Next Big Thing is Christmas, so you won't have much time for anything else.

Winter is a good period to plan and review, because without all those leaves, it is easier to see what you've got and where it is. So, in your shed on a (short) sunny day, you can work out your plans and your plant lists.

Garden seasons: Winter

December to February: the great test

If you have taken care to plant for the dark season, then your Christmas and New Year table decorations can make a decent show with leaves, berries and a mixture of late autumn and early spring flowers.

Many people do a recce trip of their gardens on New Year's Day. Most years I can muster a dozen or so different evergreens, flowers of pulmonaria rubra, a very early white primrose, early hellebores and late chrysanthemums, and heathers in pink and white.

In the garden are aconites and winter crocuses. If you have the room and the foresight to plant them, then winter-flowering cherry (Prunus subhirtella) and Mahonia japonica are playing their part. This need not be such a dead season, after all.

This is a time of clearing out but also preparation for next growing season, and an opportunity to look about you and work out what's doing well and where you need to improve your garden. But there are some gardening tasks as well.

Pruning, the big question: why?

Nature does not go about with a pair of secateurs. Trees and shrubs survive perfectly well without pruning. Gardeners prune to stimulate a plant's natural reaction to being eaten – by goats, giraffes, or whatever – to encourage flowering, and to create a pleasing shape. Not to show the plant who's boss.

Pruning creates a stress response, which tells buds to sprout to replace lost growth, or to flower, because stress tells a plant it should set seed. The living outer layer of the plant then grows over the wound: unlike an animal, in plants the important living part is the 'skin'.

Some shrubs, and climbers like Clematis montana, put on more growth in summer than they maintain over winter. This will die, eventually leaving a haystack. So clear away dead stuff first. Dead stuff is brown, dry and brittle. If it's bendy, or you have doubts, leave it. If there are no sprouts by July, cut it out. There's no room for passengers in THIS garden –

Cut cleanly with a saw, sharp loppers or secateurs, for a neat wound. Do this early in the year so the plant can recover in the growing season.

Pruning: How-to tips

Spring shrubs, like forsythia, weigela, spiraea, mock orange and flowering currant, flower best on young branches. So after flowering, in June, cut out the roughest, twiggiest branches, to about one third of the volume of the shrub. Over three years, you will renew the whole plant. Spring clematis like montana are pruned after flowering, but only if too big or haystack-like.

Some quick-growing **summer** shrubs, like buddleia, lavatera, and eucalyptus, if grown as a bush, are taken down to a 30 cm knobble in early spring. While you're at it, do the same to summer-flowering clematis. Cut lavender down to the first few fresh leaves, but not into bare brown branches.

A lot of **conifers** do not take well to pruning at all. Thuja and yew will sprout back but pines, leylandii etc. do not, so only trim into green growth if you have to.

If you need to prune a **tree**, cut as flush as you can where the branch swells out from the trunk, called the 'collar'. Don't cut into the main trunk, to minimise the wound. Do this early, as trees can 'bleed' to death through sap loss. If you cut a branch half-way along, all you get is a sort of vegetable hedgehog as weak new shoots grow from the end.

Don't scalp the poor thing, either euthanise it or trim by no more than a third by volume.

If you leave a plant lop-sided, it'll blow over. Wound paint is not used these days.

Today, **roses** are pruned lightly for a bush full of flowers rather than a few exhibition blooms. Cut dead stuff out. Either shorten branches by half, or find a bud about a third lower than the height you want, to allow for summer growth, and cut above that with a sharp pair of secateurs. Sprouting buds should be obvious by March. Very hard pruning will shorten the life of your rose.

That's about it.

Like any surgery, do little, do lightly, and only when necessary. This is gardening, not revenge. *As it is now illegal to disturb nesting birds, gardening companies will not do hedge or tree work from March to May so plan your works for late winter or early summer.

Garden seasons: Spring

March Into May: on with the flow.

The birds are mating (or fighting), the lambs are springing, bullock sterteth, buck everteth, loude sing cuckoo (actually, that's quite a rude song, if you know your Early English). The sun is now higher in the sky for longer, so the temperature ought to be rising, and everyone feels thoroughly stir-crazy after the long dark of winter, so let's get out and have a reason for going around the garden.

Spring gardens are very popular because of this, and because spring bulbs often create fields of colour, such as daffodils, anemones and bluebells.

There is certainly no reason not to have a good display even in a small garden as bulbs grow well in tubs and are cheap. Spring shrubs are undemanding, such as forsythia. But remember to keep some firepower for later in the year as well.

A Light Bulb Moment

Candlemas, 2nd February, is traditionally the date when we can see days lengthening again: this is also an ancient Celtic spring festival, Imbolg. Shortly after comes Valentine's Day, when birds are supposed to start pairing up, although my robins are usually at it in December.

Whatever the name, we start hunting out the first signs of new life and colour in the garden. We want a good early display, and for this we rely on bulbs, which have evolved to grab early sunshine before trees and shrubs leaf over.

Many early garden bulbs come from the mountains of Italy, or around the Black Sea and into Iran, where they keep dry under snow in winter, and have a brief, wet spring before a hot summer dries them back to bulbs. This is a big clue to the conditions they like: wet or dry but never soggy. Many were brought to the UK in the great expansion of trade with the Turkish empire in the sixteenth century, notably tulips, hyacinths, many crocuses, and desert irises.

When you plant, do it generously. The days are still too dark for flowers to make much impact in ones or twos. I know that buying a hundred bulbs means digging a hundred little holes, but next Candlemas, you'll appreciate your effort.

Take a risk in March: Plants from Afar

The way our gardens look today is largely because at some point, a gardener 'gave something a go' even if they thought it might not survive. Remarkably few of our favourite garden plants are derived from natives. Many come from places that are far hotter, drier, rockier, swampier or sunnier than Britain but we manage to 'get away' with them.

Sometimes this is because the original importers were mistaken about the conditions the new plants liked. When plant-hunters went out to China in the eighteenth century, quite a few never got beyond the nursery suppliers of Canton (Guangzhou). As the city has a sub-tropical climate and monsoons, people assumed that the plants sent back to Europe needed protection from frost, and humid conditions.

Which must have killed quite a few camellias and peonies, which are far tougher than that: the nurserymen had brought them down from mountains and high plains for their own customers.

So especially when looking at plants with interest 'early' in February and March, and 'late' in September and October, some exotics may only need to be tried out. This may mean adjusting soil conditions, by adding grit to reduce the risk of damp rots, or picking a truly bright, sunny spot, but if you don't try, you won't find out.

Plants from Japan

A plant which is becoming fashionable is the Japanese rice-paper plant, Edgeworthia. This has little clusters of amber or reddish flowers in late February.

Japanese plants are worth exploring as Japan has a very wide range of climates, from alpine to tropical, and often a plant's survival is not about the species, but how high up the mountain it was growing. Other dramatic Asian shrubs turning out tougher than expected include Tetrapanax, Schlefflera and even the Wollemi pine.

Japanese plant breeders have developed a wide range of ornamentals less familiar to us, such as rhoeos and hepaticas. There are also hundreds of hostas, many types of aspidistras, and many grass-like plants such as acorus, liriope and ophiopogon ('black grass' - but not all ophiopogons are black). The hepaticas would be a pretty addition to a spring garden, and the others are useful as summer/autumn green backbone planting.

Plants from South Africa

Another area with potential for new introductions is southern Africa. Again there is a wide range of climates, from mountaintop to swamps, and from plants that grow and flower over summer, to those that come up in spring.

While some classic South African stunners are too tender for us - I don't think I'll see a King Protea flowering outside, even with a warmer climate - there is no need to restrict arum lilies, agapanthus, nerines or small-flowered gladioli to pots and greenhouses. Now add dierama, large-flowered crocosmia and even a hardy gardenia, and the late summer garden becomes a very different place. I already grow an aloe outside (Aloe aristata).

And from Mediterranean-type climates, warmer summers may make fruit from feijoas, pomegranates and Asian peaches more reliable, and perhaps even sweet almonds.

The problem with the start and end of our growing season is that it is not consistent. Some years are mild at Christmas, snowing in May. This will catch plants out occasionally, especially if they have not yet been developed to resist British weather. But trial and error are part of the development of any garden plant, and garden. A little risk could add a lot of fun.

Spring in Seventeenth Century Deptford

One of my favourite garden writers, John Evelyn, has left a detailed account of his garden, month by month, written in 1664. He was a senior scientist and civil servant under Charles the Second. He was a man of wide curiosity but with a special interest in the Royal Navy, which was then based just outside London in Greenwich and Woolwich, and in Deptford, where Evelyn had his estate.

And in his ornamental garden in early spring he expected to see winter aconite, anemones (probably the large red and purple types), early tulips, crocus, scilla, hardy cyclamen, early daffodils (probably 'Paperwhite' types), Christmas rose, hepatica and 'Persian iris'.

All grown without a greenhouse or garden centre in sight. He does not mention snowdrops, though - these were less valued, although they were recorded as growing in the UK from about 1500. The later legend is that soldiers brought them back from the Crimean War.

Early bulbs often form part of a mountain meadow. They grow well planted in the mass in a lawn, such as species or Dutch crocus, aconite, scilla, chionodoxa, and the blue Italian anemones, apennina and blanda. They will spread under their own steam in a sunny place, but remember not to cut the grass until their leaves have died down.

Under trees, hardy cyclamen will flower from October to March, but they do need some sun so are best under trees that lose their leaves. They disappear in summer.

And for the bigger exotics, like paperwhite narcissi, hyacinths and tulips - if your soil is sandy or flinty and hot, they may spread surprisingly well. Evelyn seems to have grown Tulipa praecox, an orange species also called the 'sun's eye', but this is a Mediterranean variety. We now have easier early tulip types such as batalinii and greigii: try 'Bright Gem', 'Red Hunter' or 'Red Riding Hood' in a hot dry spot.

Growing his 'Persian Irises' still takes real skill: desert species like Iris susiana are amazing flowers in complex shades of brown, grey and black but very demanding even with the full panoply of modern greenhouses and alpine frames. But we now have Iris reticulata, in ice-white through royal blue to rich purple, which will come back if you plant deep, in well-drained soil in the sun.

April - the cruellest month

You may recognise the quotation from TS Eliot. Every month traditionally had a description. February was 'Fill Dyke' i.e. heavy rainfall, March was about wind, around about the Equinox, and April had its showers.

But the weather has not read the books. In spring 2019, spring was advanced, I'd say by about six weeks, going by some flowering magnolias I saw in February. In 2020, we had some of the hottest, stillest weather in March, April and May that any of us can remember, and the driest May ever.

Seasons like this can get cut off in a mighty blast from the Arctic, because weather can be a chaotic system, but there are also some underlying mini-seasons to remember. April is the home of the 'Blackthorn Winter', a period of about two weeks in early-mid April, when blackthorn (wild sloes) are in flower. (Field guide: White, fluffy flowers fading to pink, enormous black thorns, no leaves.)

The cold snap can halt daffodils and may set back growth on a lot of shrubs, but the main damage will be to fruit blossom.

On a happier note, **Little Blue Flowers** come out now, from March to May. Not the official name, but many small, blue, spring-flowering bulbs can be naturalised in lawns or flowerbeds, on their own or as mixed plantings:

Anemone blanda: Italian, so can take the sun. Blue, white or pink.

Chionodoxa or Glory of the Snow, in blue (forbesii, luciliae) or pink (Pink Giant). There's a 'lawn' of these at Kew (recently renamed Scilla forbesii)

Scilla: 'Spring Beauty' is bright blue, Scilla bifolia is a bit more delicate.

Grape hyacinth (Muscari): named varieties like Peppermint or Blue Magic are best, as some types are weedy. Latifolia is amusing – dark AND pale blue.

This isn't blue but bees adore it: Honey Garlic (Nectaroscordum) will naturalise. Tall flowers in May are brown/cream/green bells, but the plant dies down afterwards.

Don't be too quick to buy bluebells as they spread like stink. Snowdrops are best bought in pots: drying them off as bulbs can kill them.

The in-betweeners

Commercially Inconvenient Plants.

Some plants do their germinating and growing in late spring to summer, creating a big tuft of leaves, but do not actually flower until the next year. These are biennials, and very difficult for garden centres to manage. These also contain many of the biggest and brightest early-season flowers as they do not have to bulk up much in the early part of the year before they start to flower.

Many cottage-garden flowers are in this group, such as columbine (aquilegia), forget-me-not, foxgloves, honesty, sweet williams, pansies, hesperis, and wallflowers. Some will last a couple of years but all have the early seeding/first year growth described.

You can raise these separately but I'm experimenting with mixed seed sowing, as most are robust plants. I've mixed fennel, aquilegia, honesty, pot marigolds, foxgloves and some honeybells (Cerinthe major) and will put these into a semi-wild area in rows, so I can see if they come up.

Over time, the strong ones in each group will take over but hopefully I should end up with mixed clumps of plants which will then take over seeding for themselves.

If you collect seeds, then you can sow them in shallow lines - and add any annuals you would like - from March until about July. If the weather is warm and wet, they should come up very fast.

Nature doesn't have paper packets, so my rule is, if the seed is ripe, sow it.

The Spring Blossom Gamble

A lot of our tree fruits come from warmer climates, notably stone fruits like plums, apricots and cherries, and early-flowering apples and pears.

While there may be wild native types of apple, cherry, pear or plum, modern cultivated fruit varieties have been crossed with plants from the Mediterranean, Middle East and even China.

One reason was that these flower early, and so would set fruit 'early' as well, typically starting in July rather than September. Warmth in April leads to a bumper crop but a frost can lead to no crop at all.

Frost now does not just destroy flowers, but prevents bees and pollinating insects from being active. No bees, no fruit. Cruel to both people and insects, and random into the bargain.

The main problem for ornamental plants, however, is not cold so much as unpredictability. Plants from Asia and north America often get 'caught out' by frost, such as the magnolias. They are geared to climates with temperatures that rise steadily in Spring, not dotting back and forward between tee-shirts and snow boots.

The most reliable 'blossom' may not be edible fruit. If what you want is a show, then the snowy mespilus (Amelanchier lamarckii, from Canada) or versions of our wild white cherry (Prunius avium, the gean) will be tougher. Aronias or choke-berries are attractive shrubs, also from Canada, but don't try eating the fruit.

Of the early flowering ornamental cherries, the best known is the winter-flowering cherry, Prunus subhirtella, which has clouds of small flowers in white or pink.

If you think something has been killed by frost - hold hard, don't cut it down yet. Pruning can encourage new growth that then gets knocked about, perhaps terminally, by the next winter storm. Shrubs and trees do sprout again, and by June you should see some new life.

Or maybe you've decided you can live without whatever and take it down anyway. You're allowed to do that, unless there's a Tree Preservation Order on it.

Vegetables

The Burden of Social Expectation

When faced with a new garden - either new from the builders or a recent acquisition - people often feel they 'ought' to grow vegetables. They may be harking back to a family member who was a keen gardener, or simply wonder if they can grow vegetables at least as well and more cheaply than the supermarkets. And it costs very little to have a go.

Well, it can. I recall recently visiting the garden of a large, affluent home where the man had built a substantial metal cage to keep out marauding wildebeest or peasants, electrified with a car battery, within which was a row of about twenty carrots. Organic, indubitably, but probably cheaper to buy them from Raymond Blanc's garden and get them delivered by Harrods.

James Wong has a story about the world's most expensive swedes as grown by some friends - who did not even like swede.

Rule one: Usefulness.

Work out which vegetables you like, and grow them. Grow enough for yourself, not the neighbourhood. For most small-ish households, this means a few plants coming into crop over a couple of months, not the Sussex Lettuce Mountain.

Rule two: Yield.

'Which' estimate that the best return for your effort comes from tomatoes, runner beans, and salad crops, and I would add chilli peppers, French beans, and exotics - see below. Some crops do not give a good enough yield for a garden (as opposed to allotment) crop, and I'd put sweet corn and peas in there.

Rule three: Space.

Some vegetable plants are HUGE. A fully-grown cauliflower plant is best part of a metre across and you throw most away, so yield is low. Root crops like parsnips and swedes take up space for a long time, and a continuing supply of potatoes takes a lot of room.

Leaf crops like chard, lettuce, rocket and perpetual spinach can be grown densely and cut over several times.

'Heritage' varieties can be a good thing. They may crop over an extended period - good for us but not for commercial growers - or they may be too fragile to pack for the supermarkets - often an advantage for taste or texture. And they may be wacky - black tomatoes or banana-shaped peppers. However, modern varieties, especially F1 types, are bred for yield and disease resistance, which is most important for crops like tomatoes, courgettes, onions and carrots.

But one of the fun things about growing your own is trying vegetables which are not seen in supermarkets. A wide range of salads, onions, squashes, tomatoes, peppers and aubergines come from Italy, China or Japan that are certainly worth a go.

Sowing in May is not too late for salads, and there will be starter plants available for beans and tomatoes in garden centres. Look out for yellow or pink tomatoes, finger aubergines, agretti (Monk's Beard), purple French beans, wax beans, radicchio, 'Beit Alpha' minicucumbers, cavolo nero, mange tout or asparagus peas, tomatillo, dill and chervil.

Take a look at the extensive on-line catalogues from Chiltern Seeds or Thompson & Morgan. If you only want a few plants, there is no shame in buying little ones from the garden centre. Put them in sunshine, in some decent soil or a tub of compost. And finally -

Rule four: Aftercare.

Vegetables DO need to be weeded and watered.

Nothing comes from nothing. But there is a sense of pride to home-grown produce that may change the way you think about vegetables, and your garden.

Fruit in a leisure garden

Fitting fruit in

Fruiting trees and vines fit very easily into an ornamental garden and spring is the planting season. Fruit trees are relatively cheap because they are 'food plants', so VAT-free. But not all fruit is worth growing in a limited space, and not all give a good crop in England. Grow special things, not supermarket standards.

Figs: I used to get a good crop from my old 'Brown Turkey' and have grown a white fig ('White Marseilles') and a cut-leaf type ('Dalmatie'). They grow vigorously in a warm place and are very architectural but you can cut them back to a framework in winter if they get too big. Remember to rub off the little unripe fruits before Christmas or the branch might rot.

Grape vine: Sussex is now full of vineyards, but eating grapes need really full sun. If you're doubtful, choose a cold-weather variety like 'Black Hamburg'. The 'strawberry grape' (Vitis fragola) does well on a warm wall, and there are new Canadian varieties in both black and white.

Dessert grapes (muscats) need shelter and heat, but a 'Muscat of Alexandria' grows outside in the close of Rochester Cathedral. You do need to prune grapes hard in January or they will take over the garden.

Kiwi fruit: officially 'actinidia', these are vigorous but ornamental twiners with bunches of cream flowers, and are now available as self-fertile types like 'Jenny' or smaller fruited species like arguta 'Issai' or 'Geneva'. James Wong thinks the little ones are tastier.

I'm not sure about **apples**, they're cheap enough to buy. Apple trees, left to their own devices, get big - up to five or six metres high and across, especially 'Bramley'.

I do like **pear** trees, which are less vigorous and have a more upright habit. 'Conference' and 'Concorde' are hardy and good autumn croppers, but 'Bon Chretien' types (William or Bartlett pears) need more sun and shelter.

Their relative the quince (cydonia, varieties 'Vranja' or 'Serbian Gold'), is a tough and attractive tree, and quince preserve is very tasty (called membrillo in Spain).

Plums such as 'Victoria', 'Opal' or 'Czar', damsons, greengages, Stella and Morello cherries are all full-sized trees, and need their space, but the flavour of the fruit is unequalled because in your own garden, you can pick and eat these ripe. They do not like being pruned so give them enough room. Blossom in spring, and cherries have red leaves in autumn.

Apricots and peaches need extra heat from a brick wall, and some protection over winter against leaf-curl fungus spores. Not really plants for the open garden.

Lemon bushes do like being out in summer, and only need protection from long frosts. In northern Italy, they and their tubs are put in a 'limonaia' for the winter, a covered but well-ventilated shed.

All fruit trees of named varieties are grafted on a rootstock, which controls the growth rate and ultimate size. There are 'dwarfing' or 'semi-dwarfing' rootstocks, but 'dwarf' plants won't produce as much fruit. Many rootstocks were developed at the East Malling Research Centre in Kent, identified as M plus a number e.g. M27.

Easy care is important in a recreational garden. Plants mentioned are self-fertile or wild-pollinated, so don't worry about pollination partners. Pruning apples is necessary in commercial orchards, but you can have a much lighter hand in a back garden or allotment.

Shaped and dwarfed trees are available but expensive: 'Minarette' trees have a single upright shoot from which fruit shoots ('spurs') develop, and there are dwarfed 'patio' peaches. But you can get a reasonable crop in most years off an ordinary tree without special measures.

Garden seasons: Summer

June to August: The point of a garden.

To sit in your comfortable seating area, surrounded by colour and scent - or leaves - or vegetables - and appreciate the results of all your working and planning. To listen to your children playing, or the clink of the ice in a nice jug of lemonade - or mojito's - or just the birds.

If, by Heaven's grace, we have a hot summer, you do not want to be out there heaving things about and doing heavy work. If the English summer runs to form, you don't want to be out there in the rain doing heavy work either.

You should not need to dig or cultivate now. Indeed, you may do more harm than good. This is not the time to prune, either for you or the plants.

You may need to water, but if you restrict your planters to large tubs, not every day. If you have chosen your trees, shrubs and border plants well, then put them into well-prepared soil, they should need no extra water, except for new planting, or in a drought, which in the UK is defined as six weeks without significant rain.

So sit back and relax. Snooze. Read a book. Pick strawberries and smell a rose. Enjoy your garden.

Bold

Summer is a time to welcome some really big splotches of colour. Fortunately, this is also the time for some of our brightest and most in-your-face flowers.

Imagine a border of peonies, both bush and tree, irises, lupins, and some big, fat oriental poppies. Yes, you would need your sunglasses. Yes, a lot of these die back after flowering, leaving empty space, so planting them all in one spot is not necessarily a good idea. But what a pop of colour that would be!

You plant **peonies** for your grandchildren. The plants are exceptionally long-lived, although the flowers only last three weeks or so. The old double red 'Plena Rubra' is still a good plant and sweet-scented, while 'White Wings' is a strong single white.

Doubles include 'Shirley Temple', 'Duchesse de Nemours' and 'Felix Crousse'. 'Bowl of Beauty' and 'Imperial' peonies are striking in deep pinks and reds, with a contrasting centre, often cream. New colour breaks include salmon, such as 'Coral Charm'.

The tree peonies are fantastically beautiful but on a big shrub, and they do get caught by the wind. Species types are tougher, such as the yellow 'lutea' and the maroon 'delavayi', both single.

The huge frilly pink ones are Japanese-bred and not intended for an open garden, as they are courtyard plants. All are grafted so remember to bury the graft scar below the soil. Very double flowers can be dashed by rain and may need supported by canes. But you may feel they are still worth it –

Border iris: Tall border iris have stature, elegance, and they'll grow in a bucket of dust, as long as they have sun. The 'pallida' (lavender) and 'germanica' (purple) types have been in cultivation for many centuries. In 'variegata' types, the petals that stand up, the standards, are yellow but the petals that drop down, the falls, are chestnut brown, like 'Rajah' and 'Staten

These old stagers are very tough and, if someone offers you a lump, take it. The flowers are not as big as fancier types but more weather-proof. They will spread into clumps quite quickly.

Their one problem is that wind might knock the stems, so also keep an eye out for 'intermediate' or 'miniature tall bearded' types, which are shorter at 20-40cm. I can recommend 'June Prom', 'Surprise', 'Langport Storm' and 'Langport Wren'.

Lupins were rather modest plants until a nurseryman called Russell got hold of them in the 1920's and started hybridising species from America and Spain. Russell Hybrids are tall – up to 1 metre – and in all the colours of the rainbow. Unfortunately, as so often, unusual colours come at a cost to health. Russell lupins don't live long and they get mildew.

Modern types like the 'Band of Nobles' or 'Gallery' series are claimed to be mildew-resistant, but lupins are best thought of as features for a year or two. Dramatic, but picky. Of course, if you really like them, that may not matter. On a sand-dune, you might consider tree lupins, which have attractive silvery leaves and lavender or yellow flowers. These live 3-5 years.

Oriental poppies have huge silky flowers in blazing scarlet, usually with a black heart. 'Beauty of Livermere' grows to 1.5 m, while 'Turkenlouis' is shorter. Recently, fancy colours have been in vogue, so 'Princess Victoria Louise' is lingerie-pink, 'Black and White' does what it says on the tin, and for those that like that kind of thing, there's 'Patty's Plum'. These all go to ground after flowering, so have a pot of nasturtiums ready to cover the gap.

Tall

Let's hear it for tall plants, that let your kids play hide and seek, screen your seating area, conceal the dustbins (or the neighbours) or just break up a flat and uninteresting vista from the living room.

People seem mortally afraid of tall. How often have you heard in a garden centre, "I think that will get Too Tall." They do not mean, over 5 metres – which would indeed take some fitting in – but a harmless little plant growing to a metre rather than 60 cm.

Tall plants, like tall men, can be useful, fun and attractive, and need not be massive. There are manageable, leafy plants that can shrug off a high wind.

See-through plants have a light structure, tall stems and slender leaves. You can deliberately place these to veil but not block out an area or path. Try fennel, both green and bronze, tall verbenas like Verbena bonariensis or hastata (purple flowers), and frothy plants of the Queen Anne's lace type like Sweet Cicely (Myrrhis odorate). These grow fast from seed and all subside in winter. Ammi and Orlaya are attractive white annuals.

Stout plants give more heft and visual barrier, in which case the angelicas, Japanese or herb, will grow over 2 metres, as will the similar herb, lovage. Ornamental maize, which is annual, gets as big as the eating kind for your own maize maze.

Graceful grasses are both popular and well-suited to seaside or urban planting. Some make a feature of vertical growth such as Miscanthus 'Malepartus' or sacchariflorus, and Calamagrostis 'Overdam' or 'Karl Foerster', all 1-2 m. If you have a warm spot, the Italian reed, Arundo donax, easily gets to 4 metres and if you're very favoured, there is a lovely variegated form. Stipa gigantea is an effective giant oat.

In the countryside you may be familiar with hemp agrimony, which has 1.5 to 2 metre mulberry-pink fluffy **flower** heads in September, usually growing near water.

There are stronger coloured types from the American prairies such as Eupatorium maculatum, in purple, deep pink or white, and a dark-leaved type called, enticingly, 'Chocolate'.

A similar autumn plant with purple flowers is Vernonia crinita. Tall filipendulas (meadosweets) are good in damp areas. Don't forget foxgloves, for May. If well-grown these easily get near 2 metres, and come in white, purple, pink and apricot.

I'd leave delphiniums, unless you have NO snails and NO wind. Then they'll probably do brilliantly.

Veronicastrum grows very upright and is elegant, with pale fingers of flower.

I like the taller-flowered sea hollies (Eryngium), with thistly flowers in pale greens through to deep blue, but they need dryness and are an acquired taste. Hollyhocks and sunflowers are fun, but not very wind-proof.

For permanent **height without bulk**, let us whisper the word 'bamboo'. I love these dearly, but you have to pick your variety as some are bullies of the worst type.

I have grown black bamboo (Phyllostachys nigra), Muriel's bamboo (Fargesia murielae), golden bamboo (Phyllostachys aurea), and large-leafed bamboo (Indocalamus tessellatus). All make clumps 2-4 metres tall and 1.5 m across, so need their space, but are most artistic. Shining bamboo (Phyllostachys nitida) is also attractive.

The other way to get lightly-built height into a garden is to use climbers over a **framework** such as a wire obelisk. Try Solanum jasminoides (especially white), almost any honeysuckle as long as they don't get too dry, and your choice of climbing jasmine. Smelly as well as pretty. Nothing too chunky, though or the whole thing could blow over.

After the drought: Thistles

As we survey the scorched wreckage of our summer gardens in a drought year, it's worth looking at survivors, and how other wildlife has come through.

Plants that are still with us should include well-established shrubs and trees, unless they have a very light root system. After the summer of 2018, some birches were looking frail and apparently some rowans and conifers did not make it. Bedding was probably a write-off, apart from geraniums, or unless watered every day.

Buddleia, on the other hand, loves the heat. Plants with a thick tap-root may not show any distress at all, notably verbascum (Aaron's Rod, the yellow ones, but also pink or bronze varieties), sea-hollies (Eryngium), cardoons (Cynara, also includes globe artichokes), several in the cornflower group (Centaurea, like 'Bella'), and ornamental thistles.

Mediterranean woody plants like cistus, thymes and sages (salvia) should be all right as long as their roots are established i.e. over a year old, but newly planted items need watering no matter how dry their home conditions. Lavenders can be surprisingly sensitive and the pretty pink and fancy types do not like drying out. I thought I had even lost an olive bush in a pot although actually, I hadn't.

So, that's what insects and wildlife have to feed on in a hot summer. Of these, the main nectar providers are thistle-style flowers, plus the traditional herbs still flowering now, such as catmint, lavender and thyme. Out in the hedgerows you will also see wild flowers such as knapweeds , which are part of the thistle/cornflower group, and small scabious.

Thistles can be grand but they are not necessarily 'pretty'. I'm a big fan of cardoons, which are like globe artichokes with a more silvery and jagged leaf, and 2 metre stems of very big violet thistles in midsummer. They are good perennials and bees love them.

Scotch thistles (Onopordium) get to the same size and are even more silvery and prickly and jagged, but are biennials, seeding one year to grow the next, so you need to let them seed around. This is not always a problem. A striking sea-holly, Eryngium giganteum, also called 'Miss Willmott's Ghost', is a biennial and scatters 1 metre silvery plants with architectural 'flowers', which dry well.

Another 'thistle', the teasel (Dipsacus fullonum) is a seeder but that just means if one gets in the wrong place, you pull it up. Bees go mad for these, too, and goldfinches love the seeds.

Eryngiums come in many types, from true-blue lacy thistle heads like 'Picos Blue' to plants from Mexico with tough rosettes of leaves and 2 metre tall 'candelabrum' arrangements of small flowerheads in green or purple. All make a real feature in the garden, although not exactly 'pretty'.

But a plant which comes into its own now is the globe thistle, Echinops bannaticus or Echinops niveus. These are tall, at about 1.5 metres, the flowers are true globes, of powder blue in bannaticus or greyish white in niveus, and they will be covered in bees.

As bees, unlike wasps, can't drink water, keeping the supply of nectar going is absolutely vital in dry times. An extended heat wave also plays havoc with food for caterpillars and other insects. The summer of 1976 apparently pushed a lot of butterfly species almost over the edge. All the more reason to start taking gardening with wildlife more seriously as the autumn planting season approaches. And making room for a few 'thistles'.

A garden in August

Garden Visiting: For The Feel of It

We are now – or should be – in the middle of garden-visiting season, with our trusty National Gardens Scheme book in our hands, or keeping an eye out for yellow NGS arrow signs on the road.

Now we have a chance to see how other gardens look in maturity – or even as works in progress – and make mental notes about what works.

But might I suggest going further, and keeping a note about how they make you feel? A perfectly tended space may make you happy – everything is under control – or on edge – what if you see a weed? You, personally, may respond to classicism and symmetry, or find it cold. A cottage garden may seem an exuberant explosion, or a mess.

If you can put together a group of favourite gardens, you can start to see what's important to you.

Do you like open spaces, or little enclosed 'garden rooms'?

Do you need your flowers, or are you a jungle fancier?

Do you want memories of the Alhambra, Jamaica or the Yorkshire dales?

Is an eating space vital, or are you a greenhouse, veg plot and compost bin type?

I recently visited a garden which (to me) has a magical ambience. Eccleston Square is just behind Victoria Station in London, a private space which is managed on behalf of the residents of the square but has the big advantage of Roger Phillips as an advisor – at least some of you may have his plant books at home.

The square has to offer play space for residents' children: it also contains tennis courts and seating areas. But that hardly touches the surface of what has been achieved.

A calm, green space enclosed by trees tall enough to give shade and privacy, and soften sound. A year-round display of large flowering shrubs making a big impact (blue ceanothus, when I was there).

A design that leads you round the space in curves and paths and islands – or direct access to where you want to go, like the tennis court. Lawns big enough to play tag on, not so big you don't want to walk across the middle. A generous, separate paved brick terrace for parties and eating, with a pavilion, and another generous, open area set up for barbecues. This is a party garden.

Lots of places to get 'lost'. This is a tremendous place for hide and seek. A greenhouse full of unusual plants, and some interesting old sheds peeping out from under exotic climbers (I think mainly for lawnmowers, but to a child's imagination -)

And the plants. Roses left to get huge – growing up into trees, cascading over bushes, covered in flowers. Trees left untidy, leaning, irregular, growing vibrantly. Palms everywhere. Beneath them, all sorts of plants that look after themselves – foxgloves, hellebores, ground cover geranium, and exotics which survive because of the inner-London heat effect, like solanum.

And marching everywhere like triffids, Echium pininiana (google it) shooting up to eight feet/well over 2 two metres. There's no bare earth, and apart from pots on the terrace, not much bedding.

Many plants have planted themselves and are left there. This garden is managed, but relaxed. It can survive the occasional football. And the stories the children could make up in this enchanted wood - So that's added to my list, along with a mental note not to be so prissy about 'tidying' shrubs, and 'gardening' what's meant to be a personal space, not a show-piece. So, the next garden you visit, ask, 'how does it make me feel?' What's your dream garden?

Roses

Choosing roses for health

Most of us get confused when looking at the huge range of roses now available. They are big business across Europe, Australasia and the USA, and selling the latest, newest, most fashionable variety is key to that business.

But make the most of the choice. Go beyond names scraped from your memory because Gran had one. Many new roses are well worth growing, while old favourites may be coming to the end of their useful life.

There's a good scientific reason for this. The roses you buy are clones. Modern commercial roses start off as a bud from a parent plant, which is grafted onto a stock variety with strong roots. Gran's rose may no longer be a good choice because even clones change over time. Mutations build up in the cells, usually making the plant weaker and more disease-prone, so that old favourite may now be sickly.

Health can be affected by colour. Pink roses are often toughest because the rose's wild ancestors are mainly white or pink. Colours such as red and vermilion come from cross-breeding and mutation. In the old days, breeders might favour fashionable colour over health, another reason to treat 'old favourites' with caution.

Yellow or orange can be tricky. Most derive from a China rose called 'Park's Yellow', or a Central Asian species, Rose foetida. China roses are semi-tropical and often tender, while Rosa foetida is a martyr to black spot. These traits can be passed to their children, so if you like yellow, orange or apricot roses (as I do), remember to check their health rating.

Scent, incidentally, has no connection to colour. Deep-coloured roses aren't necessarily strongly scented, even the reds, and many highly scented roses are pale. Perceptions are very personal – my swooning perfume may be your cheap bath salts – so I suggest you make a note when you find a rose with a scent you like.

Romantic 'old roses' have great appeal for many people. Old-style moss, damask or centifolia roses can be seen, and smelled, at Mottisfont Abbey near Romsey, in June. Most are pink, from almost white to carmine. Many have names like 'Gloire de France' and 'Fantin-Latour' - unsurprisingly, as many are French.

Now, Sussex and Hampshire are warm and sunny by UK standards, but not as hot as France, and this can affect how generously 'old roses' flower. It's also worth knowing that in wet summers, 'old roses' with loads of petals may become a soggy mess and never open properly. And many only flower in June.

All reasons to give modern roses a place, too.

Modern roses, a selection

Today's breeders recognise that people want a rose that grows well in average conditions, flowers for a long time, does not need spraying, and has a pleasant fragrance.

British breeders include Harkness ('City of London', 'Southampton'), Fryers ('Warm Wishes') and Dickson ('Tequila Sunrise').

Northern European breeders include Poulsen of Denmark ('Bonica', 'Chinatown') and German company Kordes ('Royal William').

Peter Beales and David Austin breed many fashionable old-style flowers in the UK, although the bushes are not always very hefty. Below are some reliable modern roses: I grow these myself or know gardens where they do well.

White:
'Kent': ground cover type, spreading
'Flower Carpet White': 30-50 cm tall, spreading
'Princess of Wales': good scent, clusters of flowers
'Iceberg': likes a warm spot, don't prune too hard.

Pink:
'Valentine Heart': pale, bombproof
'You're Beautiful': mid-pink, elegant, generous
'Sexy Rexy': pale to mid pink, tough
'Renaissance': pale, good scent
'Birthday Girl': white edged with red
'Queen of Sweden': upright, a good hedge

Red:
'Abraham Lincoln': classic shape, some scent
'The Times': robust bush, no scent
'LD Braithwaite': very double, scented
'Fisherman's Friend': does NOT smell like the cough drop
'Loving Memory': widely recommended.

Yellow/orange
'Just Joey': big, frilly, apricot, in-yer-face
'Elina': tall bush, huge lemon flowers
'Lady of Shallott': peach, reliable
'Lady Emma Hamilton': apricot, 'old fashioned'

'Mountbatten': tall, deep yellow

Lavender or 'blue' roses tend to be weaker, as are greens, browns or beige. You're a long way from natural colours, usually meaning a compromise on vigour, so use for cut flowers but don't expect a big garden display.

For walls and fences, new ramblers like 'Malvern Hills' flower more than once and don't get mildew like old varieties. But also look at 'hybrid musks' like 'Buff Beauty' or 'Cornelia', and patio climbers like 'Warm Welcome' or 'Star Performer'. ('Mermaid' is lovely, but only if you garden in armour).

Now for my wild card choice. Single roses are graceful, elegant, and bee-friendly. Try 'Mrs Oakley Fisher', 'Dusky Maiden' or new varieties like 'The Alexandra Rose', 'Summer Wine', 'Morning Mist' and 'Kew Gardens'.

But don't Roses get disease?

In the smaller garden, roses have to pull their weight the same as any other plant. They are also usually much healthier and more attractive when grown in company, rather than ghettoised into beds and borders - and is entirely possible to have an attractive, colourful garden without roses.

Roses, as a group, have several disadvantages that are worth considering, before dashing out for a job lot of 'Evelyn Fison'. Most of the roses which are commonly available and well-known are heavily cross-bred hybrids, that is, hybrid teas and floribundas (or single and cluster-flowered, in the latest change of style). Those that are best-known, such as 'Evelyn Fison', have been on the market for many years.

Both these factors tend to make the rose more susceptible to disease. Unless you want to spend your summers covered in a mist of noxious chemicals, it is worth considering why this is and how this can be avoided.

To obtain the very wide range of colours in the modern rose, particularly the apricots and oranges that are so popular, as we noted before, modern roses have a large strain of Rosa foetida. This comes from the deserts of Central Asia and, as might be expected, does not like the cool damp English climate. Rosa foetida is very susceptible to fungus diseases, particularly black spot, and this has been passed on to many of its offspring.

The age of the variety also has a bearing. A variety such as 'Peace' is propagated from a single plant. All the plants of 'Peace' in the world are, strictly speaking, clones of the original, as released commercially in 1947.

But even clones do not remain fixed. There is a certain amount of genetic changing-around over time, which affects the roses used as stock plants for propagation. Many of the genetic changes are for the worse.

A variety like 'Peace' may gradually get weaker and more prone to disease over the years. Roses that were not too robust to begin with, like 'Super Star', which has the black-spot susceptibility that could be expected from its brilliant orange colour, are now practically ungrowable.

Some roses deteriorate more rapidly than others. Many lilac-tinged varieties introduced in the Sixties and Seventies are already fading out.

There are exceptions to both these cases, of course. Some very old varieties have the constitution of a pack-mule, and there are disease-resistant yellow roses, but they have to be sought out, and they may not have familiar names.

Aged roses

If you move into a house which has been there for some time, you will undoubtedly find a gigantic, ferociously thorny monster, with a trunk like a small tree, or even a thicket of the things, in an inconvenient place. What to do?

Hasten slowly. You may have inadvertently come upon the last specimen of a valuable old variety. Rectory gardens and old church-yards have been the source of rediscovery of many interesting old varieties. Let the monsters flower for a season, and then decide.

If, during that season, they appear to have caught every disease known to man and then some, it is safe and even desirable to root them out. If you have decided that you rather like them, then try cutting them back to manageable proportions.

But sentiment alone is never a reason for hanging on to a plant beyond its natural lifespan and, for most modern roses, that is twenty-five years at most.

If you decide to have them out, do not assume that you can replace them with new roses on the same plot of land. Nobody is quite sure why, but roses belong to a group of plants where viruses or mineral deficiencies build up in the soil where they are grown. This means that new roses may fail and die if planted where old ones were growing.

So that's the bad news about roses. Of course, you will still want them. Roses provide blocks of colour – especially in the red spectrum – throughout the summer.

Roses are one of the few reliable sources of colour and scent right from May into October, although be aware that even 'perpetual' flowerers need a couple of week's rest in mid-season. So, having rounded up all the disadvantages, what kinds of roses should you grow?

The answer is that the choice is still surprisingly large. Modern varieties are now actively bred for disease resistance, especially those from Scottish, Danish or German growers, while species and near-species roses are mainly as tough as a nail.

Species roses

Species or wild roses, and varieties not far removed from their original parents, have some great advantages over the hybrids as they retain their natural vigour and disease resistance.

In my own gardens, in several seasons when black spot and mildew have been particularly bad, while my hybrid teas have lost every leaf, the species roses growing beside or even touching them have hardly shown a trace of disease.

Species roses are also much less demanding when it comes to pruning. If you want to keep them in bounds or take out some dead wood, you can, but this is not a requirement. You do not even need to dead-head. Most put on a fine display of hips in the autumn.

Their main disadvantages, in many eyes, are that most only flower once at midsummer, and the flowers themselves do not achieve the dinner-plate dimensions of modern exhibition roses. They can also be rangy-looking shrubs, since there are few of patio or dwarf proportions. But they are the nearest things yet found to a trouble-free rose. I am an enthusiast.

Spring species roses are mainly yellow, derived from Chinese species like Rosa hugonis: 'Canary Bird' and 'Cambridge' stand out, with ferny green leaves, flowers of 3 cm or so across, and they can make reasonably dense hedges. 'Maigold' and 'Fruhlensgold' are large-flowered but quite gangling. All spring roses flower once only.

Some roses are not grown primarily for their flowers. Chief among these is Rosa glauca, the purple-leaved rose. This does have small cerise flowers in summer, but the main point of the plant is its foliage, which varies from a leaden grey to almost mauve, depending on position. A very striking bush, Rosa glauca grows to around four feet/1.2 metres. I had one combined with Iris pallida and the three-coloured bugle (Ajuga), making a grey, pink and lavender patch.

Rugosa roses should be mentioned here, since they are a distinct Japanese species that have not been much interbred. These are the 'wonder rose hedging' offered in newspapers, and they do indeed flower much of the summer. They have a strong Turkish-delight scent, following on with tomato-sized and coloured hips. They are very thorny and can get very, very big.

The original colour is cerise pink, but 'Alba' is one of the purest whites that can be found in a rose. The double 'Blanc Double de Coubert' retains that clarity and flowers for longer, but like most double flowers sets no seed and therefore has no hips. A more definite pink than the species is found in 'Frau Dagmar Hastrup'. For crimson, choose 'Roseraie de l'Hay'. 'Agnes' is an interesting creamy-yellow.

Of the other, large-growing shrub roses I have also grown Rosa moyesii, which has Tudor-rose shaped flowers in red or deep pink, although this does get very large and is a sparse-growing plant.

Others worth considering, if you have the room for shrubs that normally reach over two metres in height and width, include 'Golden Wings' (yellow), 'Nevada' (white), 'Fred Loads' (red) and 'Complicata' (pink, single, summer only).

If you have a tall, south-facing wall in the southern half of the country, there are few better roses than the evergreen Rosa banksia lutea, which carries masses of small flowers in a lovely soft pale yellow in May, or the rarer white form, Rosa banksia alba.

However, unless you have a particularly large tree, barn, mansion or island to cover, it is best to avoid the white 'filipes' roses, 'Seagull', 'Bobbie James', 'Wedding Day', 'Kiftsgate' or 'Rambling Rector'. All are jungle giants at heart.

Garden seasons: Autumn

September to November: warmth and harvest.

The days may be getting shorter but the sun's heat has built up in the atmosphere over the summer, and the weather is often more settled than earlier in the year In mid-October comes 'St Martin's Little Summer', or Indian summer. In northern Europe, the name is 'old woman's summer' or 'St Brigit's summer'.

In calm, still, warm days, the sun's low light angle makes cerise, red or orange flowers like dahlias and sub-tropical bedding glow especially bright. Flowers from warm places, and in warm colours, predominate: red-hot pokers, dahlias and fuchsias from South Africa, Mexico and further south in Latin America such as Peru and Bolivia – and as you might guess, none of these like a frost, so they need a little extra care.

Prairie daisies from North America such as rudbeckias will be adding bright yellows and purples. Ornamental grasses will show their seed-heads. Then there will be Michaelmas daisies and the autumn bulbs such as nerines and autumn crocus.

Your birds might like the grass-heads but they will be far more interested in your berries, as these are the calories that will get them through the winter. The reds and yellows these bring to the scene will rapidly end up inside your blackbirds and pigeons, so enjoy them while you can.

Trees, to please

Who can fit a tree into a small modern garden? If it's not just your sausages that are frying under the summer sun, that could well be you. Trees bring shade, vital for most gardens in summer. They make a garden seem grander and greener, more of a glade, less of an exercise yard.

Nobody wants a huge oak tree outside the back door, but drawing the eye up, as well as down or across, will increase the sense of space in any garden. We all have a thousand miles of sky.

Trees also, and by no means least, create a microclimate. They filter winds, keeping a garden warmer in winter and moister in summer, partly by preventing the soil from baking but also because their leaves are losing moisture (transpiring) in the growing season.

Now is the time to consider where you want your tree, as October is the best time to plant, and you'll want to look around first. There is no need to 'garden' trees as if chosen well (i.e. the right size, for the right place) and in good health, they should not need much looking after.

Trees that grow new leaves in spring (deciduous) are best for dappled shade as evergreens can be 'heavy'. All the trees below are of manageable size, under 6 metres tall, easy to grow, lightly built, and should not take up large amounts of water, or wreck your foundations.

But plant them at least 5 metres from your house.

Small trees for modern gardens include silver **birch**, Betula pendula, weeping forms such as Betula tristis and Betula youngii, or fern-leaved Betula dalecarlica. White-stemmed birch, Betula utilis, looks terrific in winter.

The **rowan**, Sorbus aucuparia, has ferny leaves, white blossom and orange berries. Good fruiting varieties include 'Embley', Sorbus sargentiana and 'Pink Pearl'. Divided-leaved varieties include 'Chinese Lace' and Sorbus laciniata.

Crab apples, Malus, are pretty, but some are very apt to catch scab or mildew, especially those with dark purple leaves. 'Golden Hornet' and 'John Downie' are reliable, with good crops of crab apples (for apple jelly). Or try 'Evereste', 'Gorgeous', or 'Red Jade.'

Choices in **flowering trees** include hawthorn, laburnum, and exotics like the 'Pride of India', Koelreuteria, or the Judas tree, Cercis silquastrum. Magnolias can get to massive proportions but stellata types are smaller and quicker to flower.

Traditional flowering **cherries** can get overpoweringly large. Manageable types include Christmas cherry, Prunus subhirtella, or the Tibetan cherry with polished bark, Prunus serrula.

For **silver foliage**, the silver pear is nearly always seen as a small weeping tree (Pyrus salicifolia). The oleaster (Eleagnus angustifolia) is similar although needs sun. Olives thrive on the coast and in warm city gardens.

If your soil is acid-ish, **maples** can do well. Look for snake-barks, Acer griseum, and Japanese maples, Acer japonicum and palmatum.

Catalpas, the Indian Bean Trees, eventually get huge but the golden or purple-leaved sorts are less vast. All have large heart-shaped leaves and white spires of flowers.

The golden-leaved **acacia**, Robinia 'Frisia', is very pretty but thorny and tends to sucker, so keep her in bounds. Also has a habit of occasionally dying back and losing branches.

But the king of foliage trees has to be the **fig**. This appreciates a warm wall, and can be pruned hard in winter. Fruit ripens in July-August: the second crop does not ripen outdoors in the UK. Get your slave to serve your figs with goat's cheese and honey.

Unless you have acres, please don't plant a weeping willow. They suck up water like Dracula draining a maiden's neck.

Berries by colour

Together with colourful autumn leaves, berries make gardens flash with brilliance at a time when they could just look soggy. As well as making a pretty picture, berries and fruits of all kinds are vital to birds and animals to get them through the winter.

But let's stand on one misapprehension now. Plants don't 'know' if a hard winter is coming, they berry in response to flowering conditions the previous spring, and how warm and wet the summer has been.

Many of the brightest berries belong to plants in the botanical group including roses (Rosaceae). This group includes pyracantha, but also apples, cotoneasters, rowans and hawthorns. These mainly lose their leaves in winter, but berries can hang on into late spring.

Berries are designed to be appetizing to birds, who gobble the seeds inside whole and deposit them from their guts. So berries are usually in colours that birds find attractive, notably red, orange and yellow. Red is preferred above all, meaning that you may need to choose between feeding birds and a long-lasting display. Up to you.

Red berries are notable on holly - all female kinds, but especially 'Golden King' and 'Blue Angel', and also female skimmias. You will need a non-fruiting male to get berries, however.

Among crab-apples, the so-called Siberian crabs have purple leaves and deep red fruit, but they can get mildew. Reliable red-fruited varieties, which also make nice apple jelly, include 'Evereste' (named after a lady called Eve Reste, not a mountain) and old favourite 'John Downie'.

Most European rowans and whitebeams have red or orange berries; look out for 'Embley' or 'Jermyns'. The best pyracanthas not only have lots of fruit but are resistant to apple scab and fireblight, which can kill a tree and spread to commercial orchards. Look for 'Concha' and 'Navaho'.

Some roses can have impressive hips, from big, red and fleshy, like Rosa rugosa, to loads of little currant-like berries, like 'Felicia' or 'Cornelia'.

In **yellow**, there are yellow pyracanthas, crab apples ('Butterball' or 'Golden Hornet') and yellow-berried holly and even ivy (so-called Poet's Ivy).

Rowans include 'Joseph Rock' and 'Wisley Gold'. One of the brightest orange seed displays is from an iris, the Gladwyn (Iris foetidissima), which is as tough as old boots.

White and pastel berries are less common, although tatty outbreaks of wild snowberry can be found in many old gardens.

For more refined tastes, Chinese rowans such as Sorbus hupehensis come in shades of white or pink, and there are tidier snowberry relatives like 'Magic Berry' and 'White Hedge'.

Birds and animals often like **black or purple** fruit such as elderberries, privet, blackberries, mahonia, and many wild plums, damsons or cherries. Ivy berries are naturally black, and add interesting shapes to your Christmas wreath. So do ornamental grapes like 'Brandt'.

Oddball colours can impress the neighbours. The bush with lots of little lilac bead-like berries is Callicarpa 'Profusion', from China. You can even get bright true blue, in Dianellas from New Zealand (rather like small rushes) or the extraordinary Chinese bean tree, which has pods like royal blue broad beans after a few years (Decaisnea).

None of the plants above are poisonous (although not necessarily tasty), so can be planted with a clear conscience in a family garden.

Planning your space

The paper garden

Drawing up a plan is worthwhile for any garden, no matter how small, because putting a plan on paper helps you to think more freely about what you want or need. You need not be constrained by what you can see at the moment.

A plan shows the size of your plot but also the relationship of major structures, like paths, patio's, greenhouses, ponds, summerhouses and trees.

A good plan will show if these are in the right position (the structures, not the trees). If you have mature trees and they are in good health and not near the house foundations, leave them where they are and work round them.

Plotting will also help to calculate how many plants you will need to obtain or buy, when you come to planting out.

And as this is an exercise in imagination, once you've done all the measuring out, you need not be constrained on your paper plan by what everybody else has done, or what you did last time, or what's there now.

Use your sense of freedom to arrange your space. What do you need, and what do you want? Think big.

Plotting your plot

You may already have an accurate plan as part of your house's papers, but for those who do not, or who have an irregularly shaped garden into the bargain, it is time to refresh our long-neglected geometry.

(Big sigh. I know. But this is what geometry was actually designed to do, as in 'measuring land', not all that stuff about angles).

You will need a long, 10 metre plus tape-measure, preferably metal, a ruler and a protractor: borrow one from the kids, or buy a cheap one. And a piece of squared or graph paper.

Start by measuring the length of the boundary that faces your garden – usually, the one including your house.

It doesn't really matter if you use feet or metres, but metres make the calculations easier.

If one of your side boundaries is at right angles/on the square to the house, measure that next, or set up a 'square' and measure down the garden to the bottom using that as a guide (don't panic - see the Egyptian way below). A very long garden can be measured in sections.

The next step depends on how many boundaries you have. If the garden is a basic rectangle or trapeze-shaped, you have four. After measuring the base boundary, measure the boundaries on right and left and note their length. In a small to medium sized garden or section, also measure cross-wise from corner to corner in each direction, like the Scottish flag.

Now measure how wide the far boundary of the garden is. On the piece of graph-paper, draw a line in scale showing the length of the boundary beside the house, the line to the bottom of the garden, and the right and left boundaries.

Measure out the cross-wise length from the corner of the house boundary towards the far corner on the right, and again on the left. Mark approximately where the cross-measures cut across the boundaries.

From the other end of the line at the bottom, measure out the width of the furthest, bottom boundary. See where that crosses over the side marks you have just made. Now draw in the right and left sides.

The side lengths and cross-lengths should match your measurements, in scale.

If the garden does not have a right-angled boundary, again start by measuring the house wall. Lay a right-angled line out from the house as far as possible down the longest part of the garden.

Wherever the boundary changes direction or angle, or every two or three metres if curvy, take a measurement at right angles to that line.

Back at the piece of paper, measure out the length of these right-angled lines, mark where they end, and then join the dots. Even if the boundary is curved or irregular, you can get a good enough plan for your purposes this way.

If the garden turns a corner, or suddenly gets wide or narrow, you can treat each section as a new piece to plan and treat accordingly.

Digression to the Egyptians

Marking up straight lines, right angles and triangles is easy if you make some simple aids. You will need some garden canes.

To make a set-square, take three garden canes which you cut to three, four and five feet long, or 100 cm/133 cm/166 cm. Join them together at the ends in a triangle with some wire. And there you are. Magic. You have a triangle with one right angle, 90 degrees, one angle at 40 degrees and one at 50 degrees.

For a triangle with equal sides, take three three-foot/1-metre canes, and tie them together at the ends. Each angle is 60 degrees. If you put six of these triangles together you have a hexagon, or roughly a circle.

The Egyptians built pyramids using no more than this. You may, if you wish, wear a T-shirt with 'Imhotep rules!'* during the measuring process, as a homage. *This is a reference to Imhotep the civil engineer, the first 'commoner' portrayed in a statue in Egyptian history (see him at the British Museum). Not the big South African bloke in the horror film.

Laying out: Shapes and scale

That's all the map-making for the moment. The paper plan is prepared, the compass directions have been marked (haven't they? You can always check on Google Earth). Now you can plan your garden.

While you have been trotting around the garden with your tape-measure and bits of cane, no doubt to the great amusement of the neighbours (or who are so thoroughly spooked by the Imhotep T-shirt that they think you're building the Great Pyramid, or possible a Masonic lodge) you did remember to mark up features which are already there, like patios and big trees, didn't you? Good. And have you marked the structures you cannot or do not want to move?

Start by aiming for all new structural features – terraces, steps, ponds, beds - to be at least one metre across or long. After that, go up by half-metres. Anything less than a metre, whether a pond, a flower-border, or a lawn will be fiddly and look indecisive. An access path can be only 60 cm wide, but no less.

Long, narrow, awkward

What if you have a narrow plot? Many town gardens are just over three metres across which only gives you potential room for at most, three types of space. This is true, but in a confined area the need to think big is even more important than a large one.

Narrow gardens will look narrower yet if they are laid out in long parallel lines, rather like dressing a tall thin person in pinstripes.

The aim in a narrow garden is to draw the eye across in zig-zags to fool it into reading the plot as wider and more spacious. Think Scottish flag, again. In a long garden, it usually helps to divide the area into sections, so that your line of sight is broken by incident as you move down the garden.

Placing major features such statues, seats, trees, pergolas or water features away from the central line of the garden will also increase the feeling of 'journey' as they will encourage you to wander rather than route-march.

A few big features will look comfortable, a Malthusian struggle at knee height among a myriad dwarf plants will not.

Most gardens have a desirable view, and some ugly ones. It makes sense to draw the eye, by using the lines of your design, to the good view. Whether you hanker after French formality or the English cottage style, keep the basic lines of your design as simple as possible.

If you want to use curves, use big ones, based at least on the curvature of a one-metre radius. A good way to lay this out on the ground is to use a stiff-ish garden hose, which will naturally fall into a gentle large curve and refuse to be twisted into little squiggles.

Purely informal gardens such as cottage gardens are often based on curves, but any area with formality needs a geometric underpinning.

The most successful geometric garden plans are simple combinations of squares, rectangles, triangles and circles.

Simple shapes

Simple shapes are not only better from a design point of view but also far more practical in use and for whoever gets the job of building them. Circles are easy to draw out but can be difficult to lay.

You stick a post in the ground, tie on a bit of string. Mark out the circle by pulling the string tight, then walk around and put in stakes every foot/30cm or so. There are ready-made circular paving sets. For a first garden, it is probably better to stick with these, or a straightforward slab pavement with the outer edge cut to the curve.

Bricks and paviours can be laid in a circular pattern but are, as you might imagine, quite fiddly. Or lay a ring of concrete, put in an edge of bricks or cobbles, put down some landscape fabric and fill the centre with shingle (or even crazy paving. Hey, I'm not the style police. You might like the effect).

Rectangles and squares are simple as long as you set them out straight to start with. Remember the way to get a right angle for your area. Lay out the short sides, then the long sides, then check by measuring from corner to corner like the Scottish flag: the lengths should be the same. Do it with posts and string first.

Overlapping circles, rectangles or squares/diamonds can be effective. Lay each one out separately. Remember that if these are paved areas or lawns where you want people to walk from one area to the next, allow enough space on the overlap of minimum 60 cm wide, preferably a metre.

Finally, the Golden Section. This is not a shape but a proportion. The Golden Section is the key proportion in buildings based on classical ideas from Greece and Rome and is one reason why Georgian architecture, which is based on these ideas, looks so harmonious to us.

This is not the case in other cultures, by the way. A lot of Chinese architecture is based on the square, and Indian and Islamic buildings are based on different idea-sets. However, back in ancient Greece, a mathematician and philosopher called Pythagoras was not only setting out the rules of geometry (as in his famous Theorem), he was working on how three-dimensional geometric shapes relate to each other.

Let's skip over how he got there, because what he ended up with was something called the Golden Section, or the Golden Mean, or even the Divine Proportion.

You can draw a Golden Section as follows: Draw a square and call the corners (from top left, clockwise) A, B, C and D.

Draw the line from A to B out beyond the square.

Take the half-way point between A and B, call it E.

Take the length of the line from E to C, (use a piece of string) and use that to draw a curve out to the line that runs through A and B to outside the square.

Where the curve crosses the line mark it F.

Take that point as the corner of a rectangle. That is a Golden Rectangle.

If you want to cut to the chase, the ratio is 1 to 1.62.

A rectangular door, gate or window where height to width is 1.62 high to 1 across will look 'right' to Western European eyes. A lawn or paved area in these proportions will look comfortable and not too narrow or squeezed.

A Golden Triangle has two equal long sides of length 1.62, and a short side of length 1. A flatter triangle with two sides of length 1 and a long side of length 1.62 would also qualify. This is the sort of shape you see on pediments supported by columns in the classical style.

If you fold a Golden Rectangle across the long side, you get two smaller Golden Rectangles as a result. You will know this because this is how the A system for paper sizes works. A4 paper is the size of two A5 sheets side by side or an A3 sheet folded in half. Clever stuff.

I have no visual imagination, what can I do?

You're not alone.

Apparently, the head creative at Pixar, the animation studio behind 'Toy Story,' has no 'inner eye' either. You need to see things laid out physically. Draw out your garden plan on squared paper and cut some other squared paper into shapes on the same scale to represent benches, patios and so on. Colour them in if you like. Now move them about. I also use this system for planning kitchens and living rooms.

But how to see what it will be in 3D? Drawing a perspective view is quite complicated and although I'm sure there's an app, that may not help. But I have seen a wizard wheeze recently, which is a garden of vegetables.

Take celery, leeks, carrots, potatoes, broccoli etc and decide on a scale which makes a piece of broccoli the size of a shrub, probably about 5 cm per metre. Draw out your garden on the same scale (old wallpaper is handy). Now arrange your veg where you want your shrubs (broccoli) trees (celery or leeks) smaller upright features (carrots) and large or low rounded features (potatoes, tomatoes).

Nick some Lego for walls or sheds. You might want to impale the veg on some drawing pins and playdough or you may be able to set them upright just by packing other veg around them. Lentils or rice can represent lawns or gravel.

Now bend down so you're looking across your 'garden', not down from above. That's your view. Now twiddle with your elements. Make a note of final positions.

Afterwards you can make soup with the veg, but not the drawing pins or playdough.

Harmonious proportions: the 'right size'

What feels 'right' or comfortable? When is a terrace the right size, when is it too big?

Basically, the scale of a space needs to relate to how you will use it. If you want a little patio for your summer cappuccino, and need no more than a café table and two chairs, the space does not be need to be bigger than two metres across. However, any smaller and the chairs will fall off every time you pull them back.

If you want an external dining space, how big is your dining set and what is the relation to the outdoor cooking area, if you have one. Your area needs to be that big, plus a circulation area of about a metre all round. And a path to the kitchen, for getting drinks, ferrying dishes to and fro, and a dry-footed route for your guests.

If you feel you are trekking miles every time you want to turn a sausage on the barbie, it's too far away. If you can't cook anything without smoking out the table, it's too close, or you need some lessons (most gas barbecue manufacturers will supply these).

When laying out a paved area, how much space do you need for seating and for people to walk past without edging around the benches?

If a paved area starts to get a Horse Guards' Parade look, it's probably too big. Do you need all your hard-surface activities in this one place, or can you spread them, and the paving, through your garden.

You will frequently see massive areas of block paving in front of a house where the owner has been persuaded to have more 'just in case' five cars and a minibus all turn up at the same time. They won't. It's not low maintenance either, as weeds get in the cracks. And unless well-laid on a really thick layer of ballast, blocks will move about with traffic and the whole area will start to undulate, expensively.

Finally, over-paving can make a home look like a guest-house. How much off-road parking do you really, really need?

The third dimension: height

The factor most frequently lacking in garden designs is height. People are afraid of big things, which is a shame. While nobody would want a hundred foot/30 metre oak tree outside his or her back door, any garden needs to draw the eye up as well as across, as this increases the sense of space immeasurably.

Height also brings shade, which is vital in any usable garden in the summer. By shade, I don't mean dense dark shadow, a problem in any outdoor space, but dappled shade that breaks up sunlight and stops the ground underneath from baking (and you, too, if that's your sitting out place).

Height can be created by structures such as sculptures, columns, obelisks, or anything from a flagpole to a treehouse - within planning law, note - but in most gardens the easiest way is with a small tree or large shrub.

Height can also be used as a sight-barrier without building a wall, and this is the clever bit. Thanks to the wonderful laws of perspective, a medium-sized tree, shrub or well-placed screen close to your viewpoint can act just as well to conceal an unwanted line of sight or view, as something much taller nearer to the offending object. The answer to blocking out the neighbours, in other words, is not necessarily, or desirably, a ten-metre high hedge of Leyland cypress.

Height gives a garden scale, making it seem bigger, grander, and greener, because otherwise all you can see at head height is your or your neighbour's fences and walls.

Height draws the eye, so use it to channel views, or to create a feature at the end of a path or walk. An obelisk or a totem pole might be nice – no need to go for the full Kew Pagoda - but if you have the space – why not -

The human touch

Sculpture, seating and ornament

Some gardens are composed mainly or only of flowering plants, notably in the 'cottage garden style'. Some gardens have very few flowers, being composed mainly of lawn, hedges and trees, the formal Italian style being one.

But all gardens need somewhere to sit, and all gardens require some permanent pathways, if only to get the wheelbarrow from point A to point B. A garden with nowhere to sit can only ever be a transitory experience, somewhere to walk through, not to linger. A garden without paths is a muddy nightmare in the winter.

But artefacts like paving, statues, formal paths, steps, pergolas and summerhouses have another effect. They people the garden. A garden wholly composed of plants with only natural pathways gives a wild effect, which may be pleasant in part of your plot, but a little uncomfortable if that is all you can see.

A garden is not a wild place

A garden is a man-made thing. We decide what to grow and where to grow it, where to sit, where to play, where to have our special plants and flowers, where to have our utility areas. Even if we are 'wildlife gardening' we are still managing the plot.

That means a garden has to be a place that reflects people as well as giving space to other creatures. So human artefacts, well-chosen, are integral to most great gardens.

Stowe, the greatest and most radical political landscape of all, is carefully designed so that in every aspect, there is something human-made such as a temple, a cascade, a statue, two or three at a time. But these change as you move through, as you lose sight of a temple, you catch sight of a triumphal column.

Using large plants like trees could give a similar effect. However, the immediacy of sculpture or building, the knowledge that this is made and placed in position by a human, means we 'see' it far faster and with greater impact. We are drawn to walk towards a statue, or a great urn full of flowers, or a fountain, or a gateway. We will choose to walk down a pergola, through a gate towards a summerhouse or an impressive seat.

We can't all 'do a Stowe' and build temples. But garden seats, ponds, bird-baths, conservatories, summerhouses and pergolas, even large permanent tubs and troughs, can all perform the same function on a smaller scale (but probably not the barbecue, unless you have a very beautiful one).

'Found objects' can be very effective. One piece of architectural salvage – a column, a piece of decorative moulding, an old pot chimney - might look a bit odd, but if there is a sense of collection, of the pieces having been chosen and placed deliberately, then they become 'sculptural'.

Ivan Hicks uses all sorts of objects in his very imaginative gardens such as shop window dummies and old kettles, as well as woven willow and driftwood. On a very big scale, the village of Portmeirion is effectively a huge selection of architectural salvage.

You don't need to spend a fortune to people your garden but you do need to choose well. Is it interesting, is it beautiful, is it fun, is it worthy of being the centre of attention?

Sit-oot-eries and pavilions

I'm sure I'm not the only one glued to 'Shed of the Year' on television. I've been reminded of the need for small, fun spaces by a friend who has just built an open-sided Chinese-style 'tea house', and talking with people at Kew about their 'pavilion' pop-up bars and café's. The Scots have a good name for these little constructions - in fact, there is a competition for them. They are 'sit-oot-eries' because you sit oot in them, to get some protection from the full severity of the Scottish summer.

What you choose to build depends on your priorities. I strongly suggest a roof, because it does rain quite a lot even in summer. Protection from the prevailing wind can be a solid wall or panel, or a screen or trellis.

Whether this is the sort of building where you have to take your wellies off is up to you - but this is a garden fancy, not Mrs Tiggywinkle's cottage, so I would resist making it over-homey (and no net curtains).

The pavilions in eighteenth-century parks were for feasting, tea, admiring the view, shelter from rain, or orgies, or combinations of the above. Their style and décor reflect this, from floral paintings, as you can see in Queen Charlotte's Cottage at Kew, to the complex references of the Hellfire Club at West Wycombe Park.

Even a DIY-warehouse flatpack can be used as a base. Alan Titchmarsh created a shell-encrusted grotto out of a basic shed. Painted inside and out and suitably beautified with whatever takes your fancy, they're not 'for serious' and need not be 'for ever'.

I would also say that, unlike some Sheds of the Year, you do not need a budget of thousands. Some interesting examples use 'found' items like driftwood, recycled materials: my friend's tea house is made of mahogany from an old conservatory.

Or use unconventional materials, like sheet acrylic or aluminium. You can use what you like, within the parameters of safety.

They can be any colour. Have a look at Kevin McCloud's books for inspiration. To sit 'into' a garden, the mid-green/teal/silvery blue/soft lavender shades add definition without yelling too much.

White is bright but needs to be kept clean, while the really bright pinks and yellows need sunshine to look good in the UK. Brilliant deep blue looks stupendous in the Majorelle garden but that is in Morocco, so can look dark in the UK. But if you want it - why not?

Planning law

Note that legally, even temporary garden constructions are now under planning law.

However, according to the government Planning Portal (planningportal.co.uk), you do not need planning permission if you follow the rules:

Not forward of a wall forming the principal elevation.

Outbuildings and garages to be single storey with maximum eaves height of 2.5 metres.

Maximum overall height of four metres (dual pitched roof), or three metres (any other roof).

Maximum height of 2.5 metres within two metres of a boundary of the curtilage of the dwelling house. Your 'curtilage' is the edge of your owned land.

No verandas, balconies or raised platforms.

No more than half the area of land around the "original house"* to be covered by additions or other buildings.

Anything else, you have to apply for planning permission - and that includes elevated 'wendy houses' or 'tree houses' and terraces.

Planning regulations do change so keep your eye out for this. A shed with a floor space of less than 15 square metres would not normally have to comply with building regulations if it does not contain sleeping accommodation. Listed buildings are, of course, under tighter regulation.

Your New Fence: and how to hide it

So, you did it. It was expensive, it took a long time, but now it's done. Or maybe it came with the house. Anyway, you are now the proud owner of a lot of fence. But however useful it may be, I think you must agree, it's not a thing of beauty.

The conventional gardening answer is to grow something up or against it: but the non-gardener in charge of household maintenance will point out that somebody has to paint the thing, and get at it for repairs.

A big, heavy climber like ivy or wisteria can cause damage to fence and worker, and a thorny one, like rose 'Mermaid', is impossible to work behind or around.

However, a range of annual plants will grow up pea-nets, which you can attach to wooden fencing with nails or staples, and then remove altogether in the winter for maintenance, or simply a change of effect.

If you can't buy these as growing plants, start off the seeds in pots on your kitchen windowsill in late April or May, but get them out into the garden quickly once they are a good size. Because these plants begin growing in spring, they flower in summer and autumn. Start with the familiar.

Runner beans were originally introduced as ornamentals. Flowers are scarlet, or white e.g. 'White Lady', bi-coloured like 'St George' or even salmon-pink in 'Celebration'. And you can eat them.

Climbing French beans are available in purple e.g. 'Purple Queen' or gold like 'Golden Gate'. The hyacinth bean, Dolichos lablab, has purple flowers but is more tender.

Some tropical annuals grow fast if you plant them out in May, in a warm spot. Water them well, and a dollop of tomato feed won't hurt:

Chilean Glory Vine, Eccremocarpus scaber: Bright little flowers in red or orange, may stick around over a mild winter.

Purple Robe, Rhodochiton atrosanguineus, has fascinating, slightly fuchsia-like, purple and black flowers.

Canary Creeper, Tropaeolum peregrinum, is easy, with fringed yellow flowers on a lush plant, but watch out for black-fly. 'Climbing' nasturtiums don't really climb and I think they look better flowing out of a tub.

Cathedral Bells, Cobaea scandens, is a big climber, with big purple or white bell flowers

Spanish Flag, Ipomoea lobata OR Mina lobata, has striking flowers in reds and yellows, needs warmth.

For a tub or patio try Black-eyed Susan, **Thunbergia alata**, yellow or orange with a black 'eye'

Plumbago in pale blue, or fancy passion flowers, can go outdoors in summer, but these are pricey and will need a greenhouse over winter.

Sweet peas take a lot of watering and looking after, while morning glories are lovely but turn yellow and twisted if they get chilly, so by all means grow them, but they are not trouble-free.

If you want flowers in spring, annuals won't grow fast enough, but not all climbers are stranglers.

Clematis alpina has bell-shaped flowers in April or May, in violet, lavender or pinkish, with a 'shaving brush' of white stamens. This grows to about 3 metres, but not densely. Clematis macropetala is very similar. **Clematis montana** can give you waterfalls of pink or white flowers but be prepared to cut back by half after flowering.

Garden structures

From arbours to vistas, some definitions

So what is the difference between a gazebo and a pergola? Look no further.

Arbour: A sheltered place (as in 'harbour'), usually with a seat. The old English name is 'bower'. Arbours may be made of living trees or bushes, and there is currently a fashion for structures of living willow withies, woven together. You may grow roses, jasmine or honeysuckle over your arbour, or leave the structure plan. An arbour is usually open-sided or with trellis on two or three sides, but not full panels. The roof may be closed, or a light open structure of wood or metal. Arbours are outdoor resting places with a little shade and a pleasant view, but they are not intended to be weatherproof.

Arbours come under the category of structures where it does not matter if you leave your Wellingtons on, as they rarely have a floor other than earth or paving.

Battering a hedge: This does not mean getting physical – although battering does take work. As hedges are made up of bushes or trees, they grow like a bush or tree. They get not only taller but also wider as they get older, and they do not grow straight upwards.

If you want your hedge to remain more or less upright and not bulge at the top, you need to prune at least every year, slanting the surface so that the top is narrower than the bottom, to allow for growth. This also means choosing a plant that will grow tightly and not die where you prune it. Yew, box, beech, thuja, Portuguese laurel, hawthorn, cherry laurel, holly, lonicera nitida, and privet are these plants.

There are no plants which you can put in, which will stay the same shape, get to a certain height and then stop growing – well, there are. Dead ones.

Brise-soleil: You will see these on modern office blocks and they could be an answer for an over-sunny room or area. They look like panels of parallel rods or slats, mounted horizontally like a shade above a range of windows.

They break up sunshine without casting strong shadows, and the more sophisticated slatted type may be angled to allow light in when the sun is low in the sky but increasingly shut heat and light out as the sun rises. You can even get powered louvres, which will do the same thing.

Cabana: In UK garden practice, this refers to a garden structure made from large timber uprights, with a decked floor and a full roof (often thatched) but open sides between the timbers. Cabanas may come with canvas walls that can be rolled down and attached to the timbers with hooks and eyelets.

They are essentially open, designed to give shade but allow a cooling tropical breeze to come through. Well, as tropical as it gets in Surrey.

Canal: A long, deep rectangular pond, usually with a stone surround, or a waterway with artificial sides, usually steep or vertical, built from brick, concrete or stone. In a canal there are no sloping sides under the water.

This makes them reflective and dark (and potentially dangerous, note: if you fall in, the sides won't help you get out). A popular feature in the seventeenth century, revived in the twentieth. Canalised rivers flow much faster than natural ones, be aware.

Cistern: A closed box-like structure to store water. In Mediterranean gardens these are usually underground, to keep the water cool and prevent evaporation.

You can buy large plastic storage cisterns for water, for example if you have a rainwater-capture system for your house. They will store several hundred litres but are not usually things of beauty, so will need to be buried.

Cisterns above ground need to be monitored because they will get warm, and they can sprout algae and attract frogs. Keep a top on them, like the water-tank in the loft.

Cold frame, cold greenhouse: 'Cold' mean that there is no heating system. Of course, the idea of the glass is that this traps heat and keeps the wind out, so that the temperature inside is higher than outside. They are for keeping plants, especially young plants and seedlings, warm.

Cold frames are wooden or metal structures glazed with glass or polycarbonate, like a box set on the ground. Posh Victorian cold frames have brick sides, which keep heat in better, and the top is like a series of window panes.

In warm weather, you will need to open up both frames and greenhouses as the temperature inside can rocket well beyond plant or human comfort.

Because they have no heating system, you cannot rely on these to keep frost out in very cold weather. They give 2-4 degrees Centigrade of protection.

A little electric heater connected to a thermostat (and an outdoor plug, properly insulated) will keep a greenhouse, or closed-off area within, above freezing, but it is a good idea to insulate with bubble-wrap or similar, to keep the energy cost down.

I would not recommend paraffin heaters. The risk of killing yourself with carbon monoxide poisoning is just too high. And never ever use these in a shed or summerhouse.

Conservatory: A structure with a metal or wooden frame, with glazed sides and roof, usually (but not always) attached to a house and with a hard floor (tiles are popular).

Originally a place to grow ('conserve') imported exotic plants as a 'winter garden', today most people use domestic conservatories as living spaces. If facing south or west, roof blinds make this usable in summer, or else all that glass will bake you like a Victoria sponge.

Plants for conservatories include the 'usual suspects' from the greenhouses of Holland, such as weeping fig, kentia and date palms, foliage plants such as crotons and flowering plants like phalaenopsis orchids, begonias and pelargoniums.

Don't forget succulents like money trees (crassula), aeoniums and aloes, which are a little tougher. Be aware that the big green plants may like a higher degree of humidity than your soft furnishings, and you need to water them a lot in summer.

Tropical jungle plants, of the sort you see in Kew and the botanic glasshouses, will not be happy in a home unless you mist them regularly and keep the thermostat high.

Other tender plants to try include stephanotis, plumbago and passion flowers but if you are going to grow a climber, decide where and upon what, because disentangling it later from the blind cord will be no fun at all.

Deck: Decking has its place. Light-weight and relatively easy to install, decking is a fast solution for small areas although you will still need to do some ground-work. You need to set supporting timbers in concrete or in metal housings, and the whole structure needs to be level. The timber must be treated against damp and rot.

Decking is a good, fast, lower-cost way to create a usable surface out of a sloping piece of ground, or to create a higher level seating area (although remember planning law).

For safety, any structure more than a couple of feet/60 cm above ground should have a safety rail or panels. Make sure your steps, ladder or bridge to reach it are secure. The problem is that decking must be maintained. If you varnish it, use non-slip outdoor varnish.

As it is wood, it can get slippy in wet weather, the reason why commercial decking is grooved. Not suitable for shady places, because algae will grow on the surface, but fine in the sun.

Fountain: Moving water within a pool or pond. Recirculating wall, pebble or pot fountains can be used to maintain the humidity level in a conservatory or on a hot terrace. These are usually sold with enclosed electrics and pre-connected pump.

Fountains in a pond also need a pump, which is usually electric these days : the great cascades of the eighteenth century use a mix of hydraulics, handy canals or storage ponds at a higher level, and sometimes steam or horsepower, which all works but is somewhat space-hungry for a semi.

Because the pump is at least partly in the water, fountains will also need a filter, and this needs maintenance. Electrical installations are the province of an electrician, especially when it comes to mixing them with water.

Solar fountains bob around and spit out a bit of a flow but don't expect them to send up a metre-high jet d'eau.

Garden room: A closed, fully weatherproofed structure that can be used year-round. Modern garden rooms come fully insulated and many have electrics pre-installed. They are at least double-walled and can be finished to interior room standards: a lot of people now use them as home offices.

Garden rooms are a lot more expensive than summerhouses but they should last a lot longer. At time of writing, they average about four times the cost of a summerhouse of similar size.

They may be constructed in panels, or on a frame of wood such as oak and will need groundworks such as a concrete pad, concrete sleepers or even full foundations.

Gazebo: A garden structure used to 'gaze' over a prospect. In the eighteenth century this might be a turret, but these days usually means a lightweight wooden or metalwork structure, with a trellis or metalwork roof, on a circular or rectangular footprint. Fancy ironwork structures are usually called a gazebo. An English word although it looks foreign.

Green roof: Not the same as a mossy roof. Green rooves are becoming not only fashionable but also a planning condition in some cities. They absorb rain, helping to prevent flash-flooding, they insulate, maintaining a steady temperature in the structure underneath, and they can be used to attract wildlife into the heart of urban areas, or even to grow food.

They are also incredibly heavy, so don't even think about it until you check with a structural engineer. A green roof is constructed on top of strong, usually metal, joists, coated with a waterproof primer, then a structural deck in metal or concrete, then one or two waterproof membranes, then a drainage layer of gravel or crushed rock or brick, then your growing medium and plants. And you, of course, and any tubs, furniture, paving etc. you decide to have up there with you.

The point where the membranes contact with the building structure will need steel flashings, and you will need a drainage system to convey excess rainwater from the membranes down a drain.

Sedum 'mats' are on sale which reduce the amounts of growing medium and drainage layer that you need, but if you intend to stand on your roof, you will need all the structural supports listed above.

Green wall: These are growing in popularity and becoming a feature in France and Italy, as they absorb heat and add humidity to a hot, dry atmosphere. As for a green roof, there is sophisticated technology behind these.

On a metal framework attached to, but a small distance apart from, a wall, a system of metal or plastic planting boxes is fixed. A watering system loops around this so that water dribbles from the top and is drained away at the bottom.

The plants that do well in shade are small-growing, spreading grasses, strawberries and tougher ground cover like bugle. Remember that the top of the wall will be drier than the bottom.

The watering systems must be maintained and you will need to spruce up the plants on a regular basis. Thee are some interesting commercial 'green walls' currently in London, notably at Westfield shopping centre and outside the Athenaeum Hotel on Piccadilly in central London, so note how well they survive (or if they turn out to be too much trouble to maintain).

Ha-ha: These were invented when the eighteenth century landscape movement was at its height, to give the impression of an uninterrupted swathe of grass as far as the eye can see without actually letting the sheep and cows from the estate on to the lawn around the great house.

A ha-ha is a steep, unfenced slope at the end of a lawn, leading into a ditch. The name comes from the jollity caused to the landowner by the sight of an unwary visitor tumbling over the edge. The alternative, taken from the reaction of the visitor, was presumably the '**** off!', which never made it into polite gardening circles.

Knot garden: In the sixteenth and seventeenth centuries, it was very fashionable to create complex geometric patterns in low hedging, usually box, so that the pattern could be seen from the main rooms of a grand house, which were elevated or on the first floor (the ground or cellar floor was for servants), or from a raised walkway around the perimeter, as in Aberglasny House in Wales.

Between the 'knots' it was the habit to spread coloured sand or gravel, not necessarily to grow plants. Some 'knot gardens' did without plants altogether, and were purely patterns laid onto a terrace. You could walk around a knot garden but they were as much a visual feature as a physical one.

Lap-pool: If you do not have room for a full-size swimming pool, there are alternatives. A lap-pool, which is a long, narrow pool laid out for a single swimmer to go from one end to the other (to 'lap' the pool) may fit your space better. A higher-tech version installs a wave machine to provide resistance so that the pool does not even have to be one lap long.

However, all outdoor pools in the UK benefit from a cover or roof against rain, wind, falling leaves, clumsy hedgehogs etc. and can be pretty nippy if they are unheated.

Mound: A sixteenth century feature, a mound is a regularly shaped artificial hill, created to give the visitor a viewpoint over formal gardens such as knot gardens, walks and rides. You get to the top by a path that goes around the mound in a spiral. It is pleasant if there is a seat or small arbour when you get there.

Mounds have come back into favour. There is one at Wisley, and some modern landscape architects are using them as major land-form features in big gardens.

Natural swimming pool: Your pool does not have to be rectangular and tiled in bright turquoise. You could create a natural pool. This means effectively creating a large pond, but making sure that any planting is kept to the sides, segregating the swimming area so that water can be kept filtered and the swimmer can get up and down.

I can't help feeling this could get a bit froggy. But there are natural pool companies who will build one for you.

Orangery: Even if you don't want to grow oranges, an orangery is a useful place. This refers to a brick construction with a full roof, a high ceiling and at least one wall made of glazed doors.

Orangeries were originally only found on rich estates that could afford these status symbols.

Traditionally, oranges and lemon trees in great gardens were grown in pots to put outside in summer and brought in for shelter in winter (even in northern Italy). The high ceiling provides air circulation and the glazed doors mean the orangery is full of light, keeping the trees green and healthy.

An orangery now often refers to a room attached to a house, with brick or solid walls, and several sets of glazed doors to the outside. The roof is usually solid but may have skylights set in. Effectively this is a more solid conservatory, better insulated but not quite as light.

Parterre: A level space with formal flower beds, the decorative part of a seventeenth century or Victorian garden ('par terre' is French for 'on the ground'). The paths between the beds may be grass or gravel and the bed shapes are usually geometric. The Privy Garden at Hampton Court is a recreated early parterre.

Patio: A paved area, this originally referred to the inner courtyards found in houses in southern Spain. These are intended to provide shade from burning sun in summer, so the normal British use – as a sun-trap – is a complete reversal.

Stone, brick, concrete and tile absorb heat and release it slowly, which is why a paved area gets and stays warm if exposed to the sun, but also why they can get uncomfortably hot if facing south without shade.

Pavilion: A lightweight or temporary structure, a building for fun and amusement. The great landscape gardens of the eighteenth century were often studded with fantastical little wood and plaster buildings, from Japanese tea houses to Indian tents, for use in summer and to decorate the landscape. Brighton Pavilion is a HUGE example.

Painswick has some pretty survivors and other gardens of the period are beginning to restore these structures. The Pagoda at Kew is a pavilion on a big scale. Pavilions are also important garden features in Indian and Chinese design. Indeed, the Summer Palace in Beijing was not a single large building, as the name might suggest, but a series of pavilions set in a very large, carefully designed ornamental park.

Pergola: A covered walk-way. These days, normally a series of parallel columns, wooden uprights or metal posts on each side of a path, with linking timbers or metalwork overhead.

In great house gardens, pergola columns are stone or brick. You can see these at Nymans, Hever, Kew and many stately homes. The overhead structure may be large timbers or even stone, intended to support a vine, wisteria or other climbing plants. Over time, these plants can get enormous and very heavy, with smashing results if a storm catches them.

In your garden, wooden frames or a series of metal arches are a more practical option. But even these have to be set in properly and to a level as pergolas should be regular, not wobbly.

Pleached hedge: Another seventeenth century idea that has returned, a pleached hedge is best described as a hedge on stilts. Pleaching refers to a way of binding living branches so that they actively grow into each other, so you can only do this with bushes or trees of the same species.

The usual subjects for pleaching are lime, beech or hornbeam. Once joined up, the hedge can be clipped tightly to make a sort of panel. However, in the seventeenth century, the fashion developed of allowing young trees to grow to a certain height before pleaching their tops, to create a screen at a higher level, with clean trunks below. A new pleached walk can be seen at Hall Place in Bexley, as part of the recreated historic gardens.

Pod: If you want to be 'off grid' at the bottom of your garden, then there are new options in ready-made pod structures, some of which do not even need foundations. Some come complete with solar panels, rainwater harvesting and composting toilets.

Most are made of wood and 'eco-friendly', with a range of styles from small flying saucer to more rustic, even Hobbit-ish. For the wealthier eco-enthusiast, though.

Rill: A straight, shallow channel of water, usually constructed from stone or concrete. Rills are attractive if you keep them clean and circulating. They are a feature of grand early twentieth century gardens such as Hestercombe in Devon. A way of having water in the garden without a large pond, but their shallow depth means you have to keep them maintained or they will silt up.

Sculpture: Part of the great tradition of garden design, in both European and Asian styles. You can be figurative or abstract, but try to keep an eye on proportions. Bigger is usually better with sculpture. Nothing looks odder than a big plinth with a miserable little figure on top.

Sculpture is often used as a destination for a path, or to punctuate a big space like a terrace. Think about the background. White sculpture looks good against a dark background, like yew. You may also choose to reflect a piece in water, or with an outdoor mirror.

Sculpture parks are worth a visit. They show a wide range of styles, many offer work for sale, and you can see the pieces in a landscape environment. There are several around the country.

Solar power: The clumsy gardener's friend. You can't electrocute yourself with solar power. The small solar lights which have a cell embedded in their tops will be good enough as way-markers but do not 'throw' light, at least not at the moment.

If you want stronger light, or a solar fountain with more strength than the floating types, you will need to set up a separate panel and run a low-voltage cable to your system.

The sun can be used to warm water for your swimming pool or plunge pool, but the most cost-effective systems at the moment are the roof-mounted panels of tubes, rather than photo-voltaic systems that produce electricity.

Steps: These can be tricky. You can make them out of brick, stone, wood or concrete sleepers, or use wooden risers and fill in behind with gravel or shingle. There are two main problems: If you make steps out of heavy materials, make sure the foundations are secure, because wobbly steps are dangerous.

More subtly, do they fit the natural rhythm of walking? Make sure each step is wide and deep enough to walk up and down comfortably, and of the right height so that each step up or down is a natural stride.

Shallow steps can be as hard to walk down as steep ones, although less immediately dangerous. So take your riser height from a stair that you feel comfortable going up and down, and then go with that.

A long flight of steps without stopping-off points can be exhausting. So make room for small terraces, and a hand-rail. Or, if trying to get down a long hill, consider using a zig-zag path instead, which will have a much gentler slope although over a longer distance. You will be able to use your wheelbarrow on this.

And for the sake of people like me with vertigo, think about hand rails or grasps.

Summerhouse: A light structure, usually of wood, with a full roof and closed sides. Not intended for year-round use, but should be dry enough to store garden furniture, toys etc., if not textiles.

Will need to be set on sleepers, either treated wood or concrete beams, on a levelled surface, or on paving. Best not under a tree or your dozes will be punctuated by falling acorns, twigs, and squirrels hot-footing it across the roof (they sound like a herd of buffalo). Squirrels, incidentally, may decide to 'mark' your wooden structure by chewing it.

Wood needs a coat of preservative every couple of years. Roof felt will need replacing about every 10-15 years, if not damaged before.

Terrace: A raised paved area, or a flat area cut into the side of a hill. A terrace will overlook another part of the garden, or a prospect.

Some famous gardens have a series of terraces, notably Powys Castle, where they are used to make the most of a view on a steeply sloping site. The 'Hanging Gardens of Babylon' seem to have been a series of terraces.

When building a terrace up, however, be aware of planning regulations. You can't build structures that overlook your neighbours without permission.

Tree house: Only feasible if you have a really substantial tree, and you will need additional supports. The house should be built around the tree, not into it, or you might kill the tree.

Leave room for the trunk to expand as the tree grows. Remember to watch out for planning permission, as this is an elevated structure.

These can be enormous edifices with dining rooms and who knows what, but most people will want one as a play-house for the children. So remember that to keep the kids safe, if access is by rope or rickety ladder, make sure you can get up and down as well as they can. Or they will get stuck. And the fire brigade may well charge you to get them out.

Vista: The extended view from your chosen viewpoint. Most gardens have a vista up and down the garden, but in an irregular or large garden, there may well be more than one. A fancy way to say, make sure you see what you want to see, and keep the stuff that's ugly, unnecessary or jarring out of the main lines of sight.

Colour

A Thousand Shades of Rainbow

The predominant colour in any UK garden is green (we hope). Between grass, shrubs, trees and flowering plants, green rules, unless you go in for particularly hectic coloured paving and variegation. So, colour planning begins with green, which famously comes in at least forty shades. An all-green garden is perfectly possible, and restful, with grass, conifers, palms, bamboos, ivy, hostas, ferns, box and yew. Japanese gardens in the pure tradition are all-green.

However, there is more to it than a job lot of trees and a frantic week of planting. Balancing shape, season, shade, growth, and contrasting moods and tints is as sophisticated, if not more so, than a flower border. Trees and shrubs can also have purple, variegated, silver or 'gold' leaves, so you can avoid green, although you're a bit stymied for a non-green lawn.

There are even some 'black and white' gardens. The famous winter garden at Anglesey Abbey has white-stemmed birches contrasting with black and purple heucheras and ophiopogon (black snake grass). However beautiful these are in the photographs, in real life they feel stunning but stagey, not something for all year. But an interesting experiment for a section of garden. The other colours to remember are those of your hard landscaping, including your paving, paths, fences and walls.

It is a shame to put a plant in a position which 'loses' the colour visually, such as a golden-leaved choisya in front of a deep cream wall. Still worse is an inadvertent clashing contrast, such as the same golden leaves with Suffolk pink. Purple leaves in front of a dark brown fence are similarly invisible.

But golden leaves will look strong in front of dark green, whether wall or foliage,and purple leaves need a light setting - even that Suffolk pink, if you're bold.

Why leaf colours happen

Plants with variegated or golden leaves are usually weaker than their green parents, because the gold or silver markings are the result of loss of chlorophyll, the pigment that converts sunlight into energy for the plant. The plant simply has less food available for growth, and the loss of pigment makes these leaves more liable to sun-scorch.

Purple leaves mean that the green parent has additional red pigment overlaid, which again reduces the amount of light that the leaf can change into food. Purple leaves usually need more light to make the same amount of food as green ones.

The flame shades of autumn are caused when the green pigment in leaves, chlorophyll, is drawn back into the parent plant, leaving other pigments revealed for a brief dying blaze. And that's why there are very few healthy plants whose natural leaves are scarlet or bright yellow.

Plants with bright red young growth, like pieris or the popular photinias, are showing the underlying colours of the pigments in their leaves before the chlorophyll has had a chance to develop. They, like variegated leaves, are frost-tender and fragile as a result.

What of grey-leaved plants? These are primarily plants that have adapted to extremes of heat, direct sunshine or wind, by 'insulating' their leaves. They are found in locations like mountain-tops, beside the sea or in deserts and other places with drying winds, which cause high rates of evaporation.

Greyness is often produced by a furry or velvety surface, as in lamb's lugs (Stachys lanata), or a suede-like texture of felting, such as lavender or sage. Some leaves have a waxy coating which produces a similar effect, such as eucalyptus.

If you scratch a grey leaf, however, you will find green underneath. Grey leaves are also often green when new, or when wet, because the furry surface gets saturated.

So, for most of the year, your garden will be dominated by green, varied with grey, grey-green, the yellowish-green of new leaves, and some white or yellow variegation.

You may also, if you have planted them (because they are all man-made) have the lime-green of so-called 'golden' plants plus some reddish-purple shades from the relatively few plants that are both robust and purple-leaved.

This is the basic palette and this should be the point from which you start to plan which plant goes where, for best visual effect, but also be aware that leaf colour is there for structural reasons. If you have a damp or shady garden, not many grey-leaved plants will put up with you. If you have a dry garden, leaves with a lot of variegation are likely to go crispy as the leaf structure is generally more delicate than for the green parent.

There will be other permanent colours, notably the bark of medium to large trees. White bark, such as that of the silver or Himalayan birches, can be very effective, as can the polished red-browns of some cherry trees. However, unless something very odd has happened to your planting, you will not see more bark than leaves, even in winter.

Green

Green, the 'natural' colour of a garden, is also the most restful for most people. In hot climates, green is a respite from the glare of sun and in cold climates, means that we are in the seasons of growth and hope, which makes it an important colour in many religions.

The colour planning of any garden therefore needs to begin with the green things, which are your lawn, your choice of larger trees and shrubs, and your evergreens for interest in the autumn and winter. Be careful with variegation (see above) as it can get very busy. Try to avoid having two variegated plants next to each other, as they will quarrel.

Flowers will also look much better for a green background, especially yellows and 'hot' colours. You can use whatever colours you like in the garden but you will find that even colours which clash if set side by side – like bright pink and bright yellow, or orange and lavender – can be used if you dilute them with enough green.

Some people say that colours never clash in the garden, but I'm not one of them. Even in your flower beds, consider where the green plants should go.

There are some extraordinarily effective gardens that are wholly green, notably in the formal Italian style, where cypresses, paving, terraces, grass, water and hedges produce an air which is at once controlled, peaceful and relaxing. Especially under a Tuscan sky, with a glass of the local wine in your hand.

Ah, yes. The problem. Well, we don't have Tuscan skies for most of the year. Under a grey sky, the dark greens and rain-soaked stone can look very dreary – to the point of funereal. And most of us like flowers and a bit of scent, and a few bees around. So although I am a huge fan of the Italian style, it can be overdone. For part of a garden, but maybe not the whole thing.

White

There has recently been a fashion for green gardens at Chelsea Flower Show, where leaves are punctuated only by flowers in whites, creams or even pale green themselves.

The famous 'White Garden' at Sissinghurst, when broken down by colour, is actually dominated by green, but only white flowers are permitted.

White gardens are very popular because they work. They have the calm of the green garden, but with additional freshness of white flowers, especially in the height of summer. You can add a (restrained) helping of white-variegated leaves for a longer show.

One of the most effective small gardens I have seen recently was mainly paved and planted with large dark green conifers, but underplanted with white-variegated ivies, which looked very jolly. Another had a green-and-white corner at the side entrance to the house in a shady area, which could otherwise have become neglected and ignored.

White gardens have to live with two problems. First, white flowers don't necessarily stay white when they die. They can go a nasty brown, as you will see on a white buddleia. So be prepared to dead-head. Second, many white flowers are actually albino. They have lost a natural pigment, which makes them more delicate and often a frailer plant than the parent. So look for robust health, as well as flower colour.

Yellow

Yellow in the garden is problematic for some as it is seen as 'too bright'. Again, under an Italian sky, maybe, but under a normal UK sky in spring or autumn, this is unlikely. A lot of flowers are yellow because bees like the colour.

Many grey-leaved plants have bright yellow flowers, such as Brachyglottis 'Sunshine' or the cotton lavenders, exactly for this reason. Yellow is also the natural colour for large groups of plants, such as Black-eyed Susan (rudbeckias), heleniums, narcissus, sunflowers, crocus, and buttercups, and who would be without them? Laburnums are always yellow, as are mimosas.

Yellow leaves, however, are not usually natural. As noted above, 'golden' leaved or variegated plants have lost some of their natural chlorophyll and will tend to be both weaker-growing and much more likely to scorch in full sun. The very pretty golden-leaved orange blossom, Philadelphus coronarius, can look as if someone has passed a flamethrower over it by July, if not grown in a shaded place. I fear for the new 'golden' heucheras as well, as they look not long for the world.

So to avoid a yellow garden which is both over-bright and sickly-looking, go easy on the variegation, have lots of green in between and pick your flowers by season such as daffodils, then roses, then the autumn daisies. Space them out a bit and remember that your grey-leaved plants, so lovely in the white garden, can blow a bright yellow raspberry at you come flowering time.

Red

This really is a problem colour, because 'red' ranges from pale pink through crimson to scarlet to maroon. 'Red' flowers either have an undertone of white or bluish-white – leading to sugar pink, cerise, mulberry, magenta and crimson shades - or yellow, which produces scarlet, bronze and peach. The two do not usually mix well. 'Red' is never just red.

'Red' borders (see the famous ones at Hidcote) are often in the pink-crimson-mulberry spectrum. Pink to crimson borders will supply an ample choice of plants in clean colours from spring (tulips and apple blossom) through summer (roses, peonies and lavatera) to chrysanthemums and dahlias, ending in a flourish of nerines. However, because of the white to blue undertone, they can be dull-coloured under less than perfect light, and too many purplish tones can – like too much dark green – be depressing.

Red flowers, like white ones, may not die well. Dark red roses often have a tendency to go muddy purple-brown, so out with the secateurs to dead-head.

The flame side of the spectrum can be seen in full flight in Sissinghurst in the Cottage Garden, which also has a big dose of yellow and orange to help it along. Flame and scarlet are 'exciting' colours, which certainly pep up a neutral background; the potentially gloomy Italian cypress and terrace garden is often given a touch of jazz with big pots of scarlet geraniums. But overdone, as in some bedding schemes of salvias and begonias, the effect is lurid rather than bright.

Pure scarlet is a rare colour in nature. Apart from pot geraniums, the mainstream choice is limited to modern roses, some fuchsias, Potentilla Gibson's Scarlet, some forms of salvia/sage, and a range of annuals.

In Edwardian rainbow borders, these colours were often obtained by gladioli or bedding out tropical plants like celosias (Prince's Feather) and cannas, which is not exactly a low-cost or labour-saving method. Scarlet is probably best thought of as a feature colour, not a main theme.

Bronze and peach also need some caution. Flower arrangers love these colours, but an overdose can feel like wearing particularly strong tinted sunglasses, or possibly red-green colour blindness. Depending on your point of view, a plant like Crocosmia 'Solfatare' or Carex 'Frosted Curls' may either have leaves in an interesting shade of bronze, or look as if it's just died.

I like orange, peach and apricot shades and they include some of my favourite roses and tulips ('Just Joey', 'Lady of Shallott', 'Ballerina' and 'Princess Irene'). But they are sometimes hard to place in the garden, and not always very visible from distance.

Blue

Let's get one thing clear. Very few 'blue' plants or flowers are anything of the sort, if by blue we mean the shade of the forget-me-not. This true blue is only found in a few plant families, of which the most important are the Boraginaceae, which is the forget-me-not family, gentians and salvias.

The forget-me-not tribe includes pulmonarias, anchusa, borage, comfrey, oyster plant (mertensia), navelworts (omphaloides) and brunnera. All of these have at least some species with a true bright blue flower, but none of these flowers are large. All are about the scale of the forget-me not.

Blue gentians work for you if your soil is acid and your conditions moist, but if not, most need special treatment. The blue shrubby salvias like Salvia patens, on the other hand, prefer warmth. One of the bluest, the herbaceous Salvia uliginosa, also likes a bit of damp.

Blue flowers also tend to have short seasons. If planning a blue and yellow border – a popular choice – you will find long-flowering yellow plants in greater selection than true blue ones, and you will need a lot more blue plants in variety to keep the balance going. Delphiniums, for example, have a four-week season (as well as needing staking and slug-pellets) while the yellow roses beside them will carry on for months.

Otherwise, 'gardener's blue' usually means some form of lavender or violet.

'Blue' foliage is usually better described as 'glaucous', that useful all purpose word which literally means sea-coloured or bluey-greeny-greyish. 'Bluing' is often the result of a waxy covering on the leaf and many of these plants come from hot or desert areas. However, 'blue' hostas like 'Halcyon' are happy in shade (although more pronounced in colour in sun).

Lavender, violet and purple

Lavender/violet is a most useful colour as it will complement pinks or blues, and can be used as a contrast to yellow. If you design gardens for the Chelsea Flower Show, you may use deep purple to contrast bright orange, to effect.

Red and purple is bold but can be effective, in a show-off sort of way. See the 'red' borders at Hidcote, and there is a purple border at Sissinghurst. Your choice is extremely wide. Herbaceous choices include many herbaceous geraniums, many herbs like mint, thyme or sage, nepeta, agastache, scabious, and, of course, violets. Campanulas are blue-lavender or purple. The natural colour for border and bulb iris species is lavender or purple, so there are many varieties.

Purple or lavender dahlias can be stunning, and there are many new varieties. Note the 'Mystic' series, 'Blue Bayou', 'Ambition', and 'Mambo'. There is also a wide range of lavender to purple chrysanthemums.

In summer bedding, osteospermums can be a vivid purple.

Shrubs include lavender itself, most lilacs, many hebe's, buddleia, many fuchsias, like 'Delta's Sarah', and many rhododendrons. Some modern hydrangea varieties are lilac to lavender. The original clematis species from which the big-flowered garden types are derived are white to lavender or purple, notably Clematis patens, viticella and sieboldii, and so is Clematis alpina.

Robust lavender-coloured varieties include 'Prince Charles', 'Justa', and 'Daniel Deronda', as well as many of the new patio types like 'Cezanne'. In purples, the traditional types like 'The President', 'Lasurstern', 'Gypsy Queen' and 'Jackmanii' are still good.

Bulbs are less frequently found in this colour, but crocuses (big or little) are typically lavender or purple, as are the ornamental alliums like 'Globemaster'. Some of my favourite tulips are in this colour band, like 'Negrita', 'Attila', and 'Shirley', and most 'black' tulips like 'Queen of the Night' are very dark purple.

There are purple roses but most are quite a subdued shade. The 'blue' roses are typically a smoky lavender or bluish-purple, like the little rambler 'Veilchenblau'.

Purple leaves are seen at their best with the light behind them, because then they transform from a dull light-absorbing surface to a brilliant jewel-like glow. Purple Japanese maples, purple hazel, or the purple forms of the smoke bush, like Cotinus coggyria 'Royal Purple' or Cercis 'Forest Pansy', become striking features in this position.

But a huge copper beech or purple-leaved myrobalan cherry filling a small garden – as fairly often seen – cannot help but cast a pall over everything.

Purple and black foliage at the low level can disappear entirely against a dark background or soil which is a similar shade. Ophiopogon, the 'black grass', can look stunning in a tub but be invisible in the garden.

Contrast or harmony

Single-colour gardens are fine if you have a lot of different spaces to play with, but they can be too constraining in an average domestic space. A rule of thumb is 'white and…".

It is possible to make a very pleasant space using foliage (green, grey, glaucous, purple and lime, but excluding the most vivid yellows), plus white and purple/lavender flowers. This gives you a lot of plant choice and is restful but not as one-dimensional as a 'white garden'.

If you add pink and mulberry to this mix, this creates a warm and pretty scheme.

If instead, you add yellow to your base colours - judiciously - the tone becomes bright and cheerful, but not strident. Lemon yellow will blend into the restful background, bright yellow will be louder.

Using orange or bright red creates a punch, so again, use in small patches. As you get bolder, you might try to add both orange and yellow.

Or match colour accents by tone, so bright pink, clean yellow and bright orange are spangled through the green/grey/lavender back ground.

Or use pastels such as peach, pink, lemon and lavender.

Red, white and blue is a classic combination but in this case, leave out the orange and yellow.

The blocks of multiple colours you see in parks department bedding schemes, or the huge herbaceous borders designed by the Edwardians, depend on operating in a very large space. They look great in a photograph but are high maintenance.

Place your colours according to your own preference, but bear in mind that for permanent planting, less is probably more. You can do the multi-coloured tutti-frutti bit with pots of bedding.

Drama in Black and White

There is a continuing fascination with black and white in the garden. The fashion for 'white' gardens is still strong after a hundred years, and there is a stream of new 'black' flowers and foliage plants.

White lights up a garden, especially under grey European skies, but black is more problematic. White reflects energy but black absorbs it. White shines out at a distance and in low light, but black disappears entirely if not close at hand.

White flowers may be naturally white, to human eyes, although many have ultra-violet markings for insects. Most native flowering trees have white flowers, as do many shrubs including hawthorn, blackthorn, cherry, elder, and of course, the snowball tree.

Natural whites cover a range of shades from brilliant to distinctly Brand X, so consider how Persil-clean you want your whites. Be aware that some white flowers die brown - like white buddleia. White flowers may also be down to loss of pigment.

Many plants throw albino variants. I have had white celandines, and you will often see white bluebells and primroses. As a result, most types of ornamental flower now come in white. Against this, albinos may be more fragile than the parent.

White roses may derive from a white species, like 'Wedding Day' or be a complex hybrid, like 'Flower Carpet White' or 'Princess of Wales'. There are many white roses available these days but 'Iceberg' still works well.

White leaves are unstable - every plant needs some chlorophyll - but leaves may carry fine hairs that look silver, such as Convolvulus cneorum, astelias, artemisias, and bright silvery lavenders like Lavandula lanata. Silver leaves are usually adaptations to very dry, sunny conditions and the brighter the silver, the drier they generally like it.

White and 'black' together can be found in oriental poppies ('Black and White'), and, allowing deep maroon as black, in pinks like 'Laced Romeo'. They are not impactful at a distance but very fascinating close-to. At plant fairs, look out for Salvia discolor, with silver leaves and small black flowers - but it is on the tender side.

There are fewer choices in black. Flowers and leaves carry extra pigment, usually red, so are generally purplish in tone, and need sun. 'Black' heucheras and dark-leaved cherries, crab-apples or sycamores glow red if the light is behind them. Heucheras 'Palace Purple' and 'Obsidian' are both robust, and the ajugas 'Black Scallop' or 'Braunherz' are good ground cover.

In flowers, the chocolate cosmos is well-known, and there is a rather spooky range of petunias in as near black as you'd ever want in a hanging basket. Tulip 'Queen of the Night' is a trouper. Black iris, like 'Sable' and 'Langport Wren', Iris chrysographes, and annual scabious like 'Chile Black' can be used in borders although remember to place them near the front. No, there isn't a black dahlia, but some have very dark leaves, like 'Twyning's After Eight'.

So let's have some fun. Make a living chess-board or zebra stripes with Cineraria 'Silver Dust' or 'Cirrus' studded with Phormium 'Platt's Black', and pots of Nemophila 'Penny Black' or Viola 'Molly Sanderson'. And a small, rather frail rose called 'Louis XIV'. Make a change from marigolds n' lobelia, wouldn't it?

Colour themes: brights

In the UK, our wild flora tends to come in shades of white, green, yellow, pale pink or lavender, and many planting schemes follow this pattern. We do not have many bold red, cerise or orange choices in native flowers. For those you need to go south to the Med or across an ocean to Latin America or China.

You can patch in areas of brilliance by adding temporary bedding such as geraniums, marigolds, bedding salvias and petunias, not to mention dahlias or gladioli, but those are not permanent additions to the garden.

In my youth, I was struck by the designs of Emilio Pucci. One of my favourite dresses was in his colour spectrum, psychedelic mixes of shocking pink, orange, purple and scarlet. While you would not want a garden that was a permanent carpet of these colours, they do bring zing to our - sometimes - too-polite selection of pastels.

If your soil is acid or peaty, there is a simple solution. Rhododendrons and azaleas all add scarlet, orange, bright pink and magenta to the spring scene. The gardens at Leonardslee and Sheffield Park show that. But for those of us on clay or sand, what options are there?

Roses offer bright orange, deep pink and scarlet. Look at shrub roses like 'Fred Loads', or 'Fellowship', 'Lady Marmalade' or 'Warm Wishes'. For strong pink, we have 'You're Beautiful' (it is), 'Burgundy Ice' or 'Erfurt'. Use as a punctuation mark, vivid roses in contrast with surrounding shrubs in purple, green or silver, although gold variegation might be a bit TOO lively.

In the true red-vermilion spectrum, in spring there are tulips such as 'Red Hunter' and 'Apeldoorn', and in early summer, oriental poppies such as 'Turkenlouis' or 'Beauty of Livermere'.

In midsummer we have montbretia and crocosmia, including 'Emberglow' and 'Lucifer'. In autumn the bush salvias like 'Lipstick' or 'Royal Bumble' make a good show, with the pineapple sage coming in last in November.

Bright orange flowers can also be found in many tulips such as 'Princess Irene'or 'Ballerina', and on evergreen berberis. In summer we have montbretia/crocosmia, but also border irises like 'Orange King' and a summer stalwart, the tall orange alstroemeria, which is called 'Dover Orange'. The biggest range, however, is in day-lilies (hemerocallis), flowering at midsummer, such as 'Cartwheels' or 'Burning Daylight'.

Shocking pink and magenta are easier to find, because these are bee colours. Whole groups of plants offer these shades such as winter heathers, pinks, and many herbaceous geraniums like 'Patricia', 'Sanguineum' or 'Psilostemon'.

Many bush salvias are cerise or strong purple, as are many bush fuchsias, such as 'Leverkusen'. The little Lychnis coronaria with magenta flowers and silver leaves will seed around, while rock-rose Cistus 'Sunset' is as vivid as you could wish for.

Finally, in autumn, there is a wide choice of deep pink border phloxes like 'Flamingo' or 'Windsor', as well as Michaelmas daisies like 'Alma Potschke', which is mildew-resistant. Yes, you have to treat these colours with some care but they bring modernity, strength and definition to a garden, a touch of David Hockney among the Laura Ashley borders.

Gardens can be stimulating as well as restful, and a scatter of these Pucci colours may be just the thing to pep up your display.

Hours and seasons: the impact of light on colour

Ready for a spot of astronomy? Here we go. The Earth rotates around the sun (yes, it does), but not straight-on like a top. It tilts.

In the summer in the Northern Hemisphere, the Earth is angled towards the sun by 23 degrees, so that the sun shines on the North Pole. Northern Europe and the USA get a full dose of the sun's rays. There's also a slight wobble, so in summer the UK is tilted a little bit more towards the sun.

In the winter, the Earth tilts so that the South Pole now has its day, and Australia and New Zealand have summer. The Northern Hemisphere points away from the sun, getting much less, much weaker sunshine.

Now for the wave-lengths of colours.

Red and yellow flowers have petals that reflect red or yellow light back to the viewer. These have long wave-lengths which are literally 'hotter' because they are at the end of the spectrum which is nearest the infra-red or heat-producing end.

Blue and purple flowers absorb all light except short wave-lengths. These are literally 'cooler' because they are absorbing the heat-producing reds and yellows, and don't reflect them.

Green is in the middle. Black absorbs all colours and heat

White reflects all light and heat.

Putting that together: Because of the tilt of the Earth, summer is hotter and the days are longer than in winter. But the general level of light is also much higher in summer than winter. So white flowers will shine in summer, because they are reflecting so much light. In winter we can put up with a lot more bright yellow than in summer, because we respond to the added light. But colours where more light has been absorbed, such as blue, will be a lot less visible in winter than summer.

Then there's air quality. In spring, as the hours of sunshine increase, we are seeing colours through a clean atmosphere as the winter rains have taken dust out of the air. The light is 'brighter' and the air lets more blue light through than later on.

By midsummer and into autumn, dust hazes have built up because of heat, which makes sunshine seem more yellow-orange In early spring, as a result, blues are bright and greeny-yellows look clean and clear, as we see in daffodils, celandine, forget-me-nots and bluebells. But peach-pink may not show up as well, or appear 'muddy' because of the blue overtone. Dull colours in the purplish-mulberry spectrum may look livid (sorry, hellebore-lovers).

By autumn, rich yellows are emphasized because of the 'warmer' colour of sunshine. The blues can now look muddy or greyish. Reds and oranges will glow, purples will look lively and rich.

In the short, low-light days of winter, only bright reds and yellow will really stand out, which is one reason why most berries are in these colours.

Within each day, there is a similar shift from 'cool' light at dawn and in the early morning, to a 'warm' light by evening as the day's dust hazes build up. But whatever the time, white flowers will reflect any light that's going.

Flowers that bloom at night, usually to attract moths, are nearly all white or very pale green.

Other colours will reflect light depending on how much white is in the mix, so dark reds and purples disappear under low light conditions but lemon, pale pinks or lavenders may be almost as bright as white. If you love your deep purple dahlias, place them near to where you sit or normally stand to view the garden, or you may not see them at all.

The fourth colour dimension: time

Because not everything you plant will come out at the same time.

It is possible to plan your garden to take advantage of the colours of natural light. Concentrate on yellow and blue in early spring, pinks and lavender in early summer, moving to white or sharper, brighter colours in mid-summer, then into white, red and yellow for autumn into winter.

Yes, you can. Daffodils, bluebells and chionodoxa, followed by peonies, pinks and old pink June-flowering roses. Then white roses, blue agapanthus, white agapanthus and white hydrangeas, plus geraniums or whatever bedding plants you choose. Then white Japanese anemones, bronze chrysanthemums, late yellow roses, prairie daisies like rudbeckias, and berries.

Or pick up on the times of day. Use bright colours for the furthest parts of the garden, which you will visit during the day, but pale reflective colours on the parts near the house, to shine out in the evenings. Some white flowers obligingly open at night, such as old-fashioned tobacco plants (nicotiana).

Or emphasise perspective. Put grey, blues and lavender in the distance, to make your garden seem larger, and your bright peppy colours - reds, yellows and oranges - close to you. But greys can look miserable in winter, so don't mix these with your winter bed or walk.

You can also use a spot of bright colour to draw the eye, to pull people along a path towards a pot or a bed. And that means you can draw attention to different parts of the garden at different seasons.

Or play with mood, using white, grey and lavender where you sit and ponder in summer, child's paint-box colours where you need energising in winter and spring.

So the question in planning is not only what colour your plant is, but when it is, and what else will be around at the time.

Mood, shapes, shadows

What mood is your garden?

People want different things from their outdoor spaces. You might want somewhere quiet and shut off from everyday life or you might want a playground (for children or adults). You might just want somewhere that delivers a different experience from your home or your work.

If your work is fast-paced, your garden may deliver calm and apparent eternity but if you have a boring job, plan one that is full of excitement and change.

This is more than a question of what physical features you choose for your garden. A space that includes lawn, a terrace, a summerhouse and some flowerbeds does not, in itself, deliver a 'mood'. That is down to how your features are chosen, how you place them, the colours and plants you use, and how you arrange them.

The 'message' from a garden where the summerhouse is painted bright yellow and blue, on a terrace area laid out with a chimenea and terracotta pots of red geraniums, bananas, dahlias and palms, is entirely different from the same arrangement of spaces where the summerhouse is pale green and furnished with chintz cushions, the terrace area has an elegant white café set, the pots contain white lilies, and the planting is composed of white and pink roses, and lavender.

One is not 'better' than the other. It can only be 'better for you'.

Simplicity rules

In most garden spaces, as the CIA say, 'Keep It Simple, Stupid.' If too much is happening in too small a space, the effect becomes hectic and distracting. As in most art forms, better to do a few things well than have a go at everything and make no good fist of anything.

One way to ensure that this is less likely to happen is the space planning system used here, where all features are of a significant scale and the relationship between areas of use has been worked out.

The colour planning will also pull a garden's mood together, because this will give a considered feel to your floral experience.

Other ways to connect a garden thematically are to restrict the number of types of hard landscaping you use in each space. Use stone or brick, formal paving or crazy paving, cobbles and shingle or bark, but not a bit of everything all over a single space. Paint colours or wood-stains, if you use them, also benefit from simplification and harmony.

By garden space, I mean the area of a garden that you can take in within a single glance. In a long or large garden, you can change the mood, colour and textures as you move through, as long as you put visual barriers between one section and the next. This might be a fence, or trellis, or some big shrubs or bamboo. In a terraced garden, you can treat each as a separate section. And that brings us on to –

The journey

Except for the smallest backyards, a garden of a size big enough to have separate visual areas can provide a journey. As you move through the garden and use different features, you can change the mood from formal to informal, from 'wild' to manicured, from bright to relaxing, and back again.

At each point in the journey, decide on your viewpoint feature. This could be a statue, a big tub with bedding or feature planting, an arch, a seat, a summerhouse. Unlikely to be the shed or the barbecue. A swimming pool, maybe. Jacuzzi, up to you.

You guide the journey by providing paths and walkways. Some paths are entirely practical such as those in a vegetable patch and are strictly A to B. If you have external access points along your boundary, you will also want some weatherproof paths that get directly there from the house or entrance. (NB. If you don't provide a walkway the inhabitants of your house and garden will make their own. Muddily.)

But other paths and walkways can meander to take in your features, through woodland planting or a meadow, a route to the summerhouse that goes past your best flowerbed, a little path to your 'secret' garden behind a hedge or trellis.

The question is not just 'how can I get there' but 'what is the best and most entertaining way to get there'.

And on your journey, especially in a long or large garden, give yourself plenty of seats or shelters from the rain. When planning large-scale leisure parks, the rule of thumb is a seat every fifty paces or less.

Put seats where there is something to look at, and vice versa. Remember that most human beings get uncomfortable if their back is exposed to an empty space (the technical tag for this is 'prospect and refuge'). This is why seats are often set against a wall or enclosed by an arbour.

In my suburban thirty-metre rear garden, I had two benches, a summerhouse and a greenhouse with seating inside, as well as garden chairs that can be moved about.

A journey also needs a destination. In a long garden, give yourself a reason to go to the end and make it interesting on the way. In a large garden, give yourself a reason to use each space and vary the moods and uses. Gardens don't need corridors. There is no reason to have sections that 'do nothing'.

Garden styles

Formal: the Italian and Islamic heritage

The great gardens of France and Italy are the descendants of Roman design. You can see a reconstructed Roman garden in the villa at Fishbourne, near Chichester. The equally great gardens of Spain are derived from Islamic and Middle Eastern patterns.

What they have in common is a commitment to the demonstration of human control over nature as a foretaste of a divine or perfect place, an Eden, Paradise or Heaven.

My own personal taste is for Italian over formal French design. I find the vast expanses of a garden by Le Notre, as at Versailles, rather bleak. You can see this style in action in the restored formal gardens at Hampton Court.

There is an underlying quirkiness to Italian design that seems to sit better with English tastes, and the great formal gardens in the UK are frequently described as Italian, as at the Astor's garden at Hever Castle.

Italian gardens use a lot of hard landscaping, in the form of terraces, paths, stone fountains, stairs and statues. Isola Bella in Lake Maggiore in Italy is nearly all such constructed stonework. The green bits may include grass, cypress, yew and other evergreen trees, and the vast majority of gardens in this style include formal water features such as fountains, cascades, canals and regularly-shaped stone-edged ponds.

Tubs and urns are large, containing trees like lemons and oranges. The layout is geometric, with square or circular terraces and water features. Paths are also straight or on a defined circular curve.

The popes and cardinals who originally set these gardens out were as keen on collecting exotic and beautiful flowers as any other Renaissance princes but over time the exotics died out, so the modern take on 'Italian style' contains few flowers.

This kind of garden is relaxing because order rules.

They are also simplified in materials and planting, so do not come across as muddled or noisy. The strong design and use of evergreens and permanent features mean they look good at most times of the year.

The Islamic style is less often found in the UK, but shares the underlying sense of order and the use of permanent stone, water and evergreen features. Islamic gardens also make use of the beautiful glazed tiles made across North Africa and the Middle East. The bright sunshine of these countries means that turquoise, cobalt blue and peppermint green look especially effective.

A classic Islamic garden is walled, then divided cross-wise into four quarters by narrow straight canals or stone-lined rills, to represent the four quarters of the world. There is often a pool where the canals meet in the middle.

Paradise gardens rely heavily on trees, especially fruit trees. Lawns are not often a feature because they would die in a waterless Iranian or southern Spanish summer.

Roses are important for scent and colour but again, this is not a 'flowery' style of garden. This is a garden for shade, tinkling fountains, and a breeze sighing through palms and apricots.

Informal: the cottage garden idyll

Britain has given two garden styles to the world, which are the cottage garden, and the landscape garden. Cottage garden style has a rather confused origin. Cottages in villages or on estates, when they were inhabited by agricultural workers and their families of six or seven - not an investment banker and his latest partner - had a very small area of land attached.

The cottages themselves were rented to the workers, usually tied to the job at the farm or local estate. They were not, therefore, strictly hereditary, although families could stay in them for two or three generations if the job passed down the line. The tenants were always at risk of being turfed out.

In these small bits of land, in their very small free time, most workers grew vegetables. Flowers were an afterthought. Either wildflowers were brought in (such as primroses) or the toughest plants were handed around the village or sown from seed, such as marigolds and marguerites.

A larger 'cottage' is better described as a smallholding. If your cottage is detached and has half an acre or an acre attached, this would have been used for pigs, chickens, maybe some apple trees, many, many potatoes and a patch for cabbages (and was probably home to two or three generations of the family).

But what about all those pictures of old Joe sitting smoking in his porch with honeysuckle twining over his head? What abut the profusion of roses and hollyhocks among the cabbages and peas?

Our image of the cottage garden is largely based on watercolours by a lady called Helen Allingham. But she was painting in the 1890's through to the 1920's, when cottages and their agricultural workforces were already on the way out. These images are Edwardian England hankering after a simpler time.

Marjorie Fish, who did so much to popularise cottage style after 1945, was well aware of this. In her books she regularly compares the remaining agricultural cottages and their scraps of land in East Lambrook to her own extensive gardens, and does not pretend that in any way her own 'cottage garden' is representative.

So-called 'cottage plants', like Alchemilla mollis, are also frequently nothing of the sort. Many are imported plants, often introduced quite late. Buddleia only came into the UK in 1890. Alchemilla mollis was introduced in 1874 but does not seem to have been in wide use until the late 1940's.

The brightly coloured modern Russell lupins date only to the 1930's. They are exotics, and, like all such, were first bought and used by rich landowners. But they look 'cottagey' which is to say profuse and colourful, if not very structured.

So the cottage style is just that, a style, as artificial in its way as a British Italian or a British Japanese garden. It depends on masses of plants, mainly flowering ones, and clouds and sweeps of mixed colour. There is a natural peak in June and July, so you need to plan your cottage garden carefully to carry colour into October.

Paths are rarely straight, paving is based on bricks, cinder paths or crazy paving, the mass of plants is preferred over any extensive vista, and the scale is usually small. Cottages did not usually have lawns, because they did not have lawnmowers (apart from the odd sheep) so the journey in a cottage garden is through clouds of exuberance.

Cottage style has been remarkably popular for over fifty years because it seems easy. You don't have to do all the setting out and balancing that you need for a formal garden or the herbaceous borders we look at later.

It does suit smaller spaces and the inveterate plant collector, because you can always squeeze something new in. But this style can also be messy and actually rather hard to manage – how do you get to your plants as they go over or need pruning? – and the dividing line between exuberance and hotchpotch can be a fine one. Mixed plantings in the new millennium have moved on. See prairie and dry-garden styles later in this chapter.

Augmented nature: landscape and wilderness

But what the nobs up at the big house really wanted, from about the year 1730, is to look out over something that makes them feel like lords of the world. This is wilderness tamed, an Arcadian vision by Poussin or Claude Lorrain, right outside your dining room.

Capability Brown, the canniest of Geordies, is credited with popularising the landscape garden although the idea had been knocking around for a while. To this day, in France or Germany, an 'English garden' means a landscaped park.

Brown, Repton and the other great designers were not gardeners. You will find no details of flowers or unusual shrubs in their designs. They moved mountains, also lakes, villages, roads, mature trees and even, on occasion, the main mansion of their usually fantastically rich clients.

The style was adjusted in early Victorian times, as new and exciting imported flowers like rhododendrons started to come from the Himalayas and rich patrons wanted ways to show them off.

John Nash, who designed so many Regency and early Victorian villas, also designed their grounds and included what we would think of as mixed borders. Some of these have been reinstated at Kew and St James' Park.

Landscape design on this scale is unlikely to trouble most domestic gardeners these days, although it's always interesting to see how it was done. Humphrey Repton's Red Books should also be saluted as one of the most effective ways ever created of parting rich clients from their loot, complete with before and after images.

But there was a previous incarnation for 'nature' called the 'wilderness'. In a seventeenth century garden, the section closest to the house would usually include a parterre, which was composed of gravel and low bushes, often box, pruned into complex knot patterns. The area was designed to be viewed from the state rooms, which were on the first floor.

However, the Stuarts were also very keen on keep-fit. They invented the dumb-bell. In the days without police or any regular form of peace-keeping force outside the walls of an estate, the ladies and children had to get their outdoor exercise somehow. Estates were designed with long 'rides' for horses and carriages, but for exercise on foot, both mazes and wildernesses were popular.

A wilderness is not a mess of brambles. It is a series of structured paths through natural or informal planting, which is so tall so that you cannot see over the top. In a relatively small area, you can plan miles of walks which do not repeat and which open up a series of different vistas.

A few still exist, for example at Ham House near Richmond, London, and one is being restored at Chevening in Kent.

This kind of 'landscape' has immediate relevance for anyone planning a small woodland garden or secret gardens to add to the journey through your space.

You can formalise your plan to a maze, or keep it informal and naturalistic. If you wish, you can call this a wilderness.

Digression to ancient Crete: a seven-fold 'Classical' maze or labyrinth.

How to create a maze. Set out four posts and join them with string in a St George's cross, ("Maud! The neighbour's out there again with sticks and bits of string!"), or mark it on a piece of paper, if you want to try this out in privacy first. The end shape is a sort of oval thumb-print.

1. Mark four dots between the arms of the cross, in a square
2. Draw Line A from the top arm of the cross to the right, loop under the top-right dot, then around it and over in a curve to the left, to end at the top-left dot.
3. Draw Line B from the top-right dot, leftwards under the line you've just drawn, then loop round the end of that line and curve over the top of it to finish at the end of the right arm of the cross.
4. Draw Line C from the left arm of the cross, up and around what you have drawn so far, right round as far as the bottom-right dot, loop round inside this then go back round the other way, right over the top, to finish at the bottom-left dot.
5. Draw line D from the bottom-right dot up between the lines and keep going until you've gone around the bottom-left dot, then back right over the top and round until you end at the bottom of the cross.

This pattern is very ancient. Neolithic, in fact. The earliest versions are over three thousand years old. Sometimes called the Troytown maze, it has been associated with ritual processions since time immemorial and seems to have been widely popular, presumably because the trick for drawing it out is so simple once you learn how.

Technically this maze is 'unicursal' as there is only one way round. This is not the kind of maze where you get lost. These 'seven-fold' or 'Classical' mazes have been cut into turf or arranged in stone in countries right across Northern Europe, and were often used for May Day dancing. Medieval 'classical' turf mazes still survive, such as the one at Dalby in North Yorkshire.

There is no evidence that the Labyrinth in Crete (as in Minotaurs, Theseus and Ariadne) was like this but the pattern has been used as its symbol for thousands of years. The kind of game maze where you can get lost, as at Hampton Court, is much more recent, becoming popular in the 16th century. These are exercises in mathematics.

The current UK maze-master is Adrian Fisher, who develops extraordinary mazes based on all manner of pictures and 3-D illusions: see his work at Longleat. He has written several books on mazes, which are fascinating. I dare say there are some computer programs around to help you design your own if you wish.

July profusion and Jekyllian myopia

Flowers crept back into the garden in Victorian times. Actually, in the villas of the middle classes, they had never left. No gardens on a small scale from this period still remain. In general, antique gardens only survive when their rich patrons ran out of money, and so nobody redesigned the park for a couple of centuries. In smaller spaces, this did not happen.

Some early plans do exist, notably for a row of houses at Chatham dockyards belonging to captains and officers in the 1830's, which show formal geometric flower beds and paths - but no lawns. Until the mechanical lawnmower started to become cheaper and more easily usable in the 1840's, the only ways to keep grass short were a scythe or a sheep, neither of which is easy in a suburban back garden.

Back to the rich people. From 1820 onwards, there was a flood of new plants into Britain, Chinese roses and Indian rhododendrons, conifers from North America, pelargoniums and gladioli from South Africa, and the ultimate status symbols, the giant Amazonian water lily and jungle orchids. So much colour, so much vibrancy, and so much money to keep crews of gardeners at work.

A large estate had a small army of gardeners. Even relatively modest estates would employ upwards of twenty men, some of whom were in the kitchen gardens, but many were looking after exotics like vines and pineapples, or the decorative planting.

Labour was cheap, which had an impact on what kinds of gardening were fashionable. This is when bedding out became both possible and popular. With the development of wrought iron frames and float glass, large greenhouses could be built, heated with readily available coal.

Exotics like pelargoniums and lobelia, French marigolds, salvias and dahlias, grew quickly under glass. With so much labour available, it was not unusual for extensive bedding displays to be replaced three times or more through the season. You can still see large Victorian-style bedding displays in many public parks. At Osborne House on the Isle of Wight, Waddesdon Manor and in front of the Palm House at Kew, they are a deliberate feature.

The Anti-Bedding reaction

Reaction did set in, after a while. These highly artificial gardens set some teeth on edge, notably those of **William Robinson** of Gravetye Manor in Sussex, who felt that gardens should reflect and celebrate nature, not take it for thirteen rounds and a knock-out punch. His influential books on natural gardening praised woodlands, informal groves and glades. He also helped to popularise rockeries, on which wild plants collected by the rich and adventurous on trips to the Highlands of Scotland or the Alps could be grown in conditions that recreated their original homes.

This style was also a good fit for the newly stylish collections of rhododendrons, assembled into the great gardens of Wales (Bodnant) and the West (Exbury) in a recreation of Himalayan forests. But not every home wants or needs a forest outside the back door. Although bedding might be just too suburban for the fashionable Edwardian, they did want their flowers and their summer show

Enter **Gertrude Jekyll and Ellen Wilmott**. These ladies had an immense influence on garden design in the late Victorian and Edwardian periods, and it is not too much to say that they perfected the concept of the herbaceous border.

But it is also important to remember that Miss Willmott had huge personal wealth, nearly all of which she spent on her garden. Gertrude Jekyll designed her gardens for the very rich, many of whom had also ordered a modern house from her young friend Edwin Lutyens. They threw money and manpower at their gardens, because they were there to throw.

Gertrude Jekyll is best known for the way she uses colour in her border plans. Her borders are long, to a hundred or more metres, and often four, five or more metres wide. They were often planned in pairs, with a grass walk between them. A strip of stone paving or a stone path may define the edge of the border. Typically, plants are grouped in long ovals or strips by colour, parallel to the border edge. Colours may be arranged in progression on a rainbow basis, or with brights at the centre and pastels towards the ends.

When seen in perspective as you walk up the border, colours weave and change, although they are not as impressive when seen head-on, as inevitable gaps will show up as the season goes on. Miss Jekyll filled these with temporary plants like dahlias, pots of lilies, or clumps of plants grown in the kitchen garden and moved bodily for their four weeks of show. They look terrific when well grown, especially if you half-close your eyes.

Herewith is a clue. Miss Jekyll was extremely short sighted. Trained as an artist, she only began planning gardens when her eyesight no longer permitted her to undertake embroidery and close craft work. Colour is everything, structure is what you can see from the plan, much less often in planting. She did use hedges, paths and steps although these can also be put down to the architect Lutyens working beside her.

Structural planting within these borders is minimal. These magnificent rainbows are also quite short lived. Her wealthy patrons had a precise social calendar. In winter, men of business lived in a townhouse in the city or, if your health was delicate, in the south of France. Families remaining in the country hunted in winter and came back to London in February, although there might be country house parties over Easter and Whit.

Parliament began the long recess in July, so politicians and men of business came down to the country property (and its garden) and stayed there until August, when they went north to take pot-shots at poor defenceless grouse. Then back to London in September, and running the country.

A Jekyll border will start in June and peak in July, and may not have much to say for itself later in the season. It has few shrubs or bulbs to entertain you in spring or winter, as there would have been no patrons to enjoy them. Indeed, if made up entirely of herbaceous plants, all there may be to see is bare earth. Winter gardens are a recent development.

The lessons from these huge borders and their descendants, as seen in many stately homes, is the clever use of colour and their sense of theatre, not the profligate use of labour. They are anything but low maintenance, but are showpieces on a grand scale. Enjoy them, take their photograph, but they are from another era.

Woodland gardens

Many of the most beautiful gardens in Britain are based on deciduous woodland, which is the natural plant cover for most of the UK. Many of our favourite plants have evolved to make the most of this. So the plants of woodland – and this includes the huge range of rhododendrons and camellias – want the protection from hot sunshine and wind that a natural light forest will give, but cannot exist in dark shadow any more than any other plant. They like glades, rides and moisture. Pine forests are not native to most of the southern UK although there was (and still is a little left of) the ancient Caledonian pine forest covering much of Scotland, and others in parts of Wales.

When the ice sheet retreated after the last Ice Age in about 10,000 BC, the first plants back into the UK were birch, hazel, alder and small-leaved linden trees, Tilia cordata. In the next thousand years or so, ash, oak, beech, hornbeam and smaller plants like rowan, elder and holly were established. The Romans seem to have brought elm and sweet chestnut.

In the current period the natural 'climax' forest in most of the UK is oak, ash, beech, lime (tilia), alder or birch.

All these trees lose their leaves in winter: they are deciduous, also called broad-leaved, which is a clue to how plants underneath them grow. Most woodland plants sprout and flower early in the year, before the leaves on the trees stop sunshine getting to the soil, so primroses, wood anemones, snowdrops, daffodils, bluebells and other 'spring bulbs' are getting their growth in first. In autumn, a few also try to get flowers up and out as leaves are falling, notably the little woodland cyclamens, Cyclamen coum and hederifolium. Bigger plants take advantage of the better light at the woodland edge towards midsummer, such as dog roses, honeysuckle, campanula and aquilegia.

None of these can survive under an evergreen forest canopy. Pine forests are remarkably silent because there are relatively few insects and therefore birds. They have very little growing beneath the trees, except where light breaks through, and this is their natural state.

The spookiest, darkest, most silent natural forest, however, is yew. There are examples in Wales and Sussex. Very few insects will occupy a yew forest, and the only plant underfoot is moss.

Woodland, not a forest

If you ask people what a forest should look like, most will reply that there should be a lot of very big trees. However, natural forests do not normally have many large (old) trees, because the cycle of regeneration is too rapid.

If you look at a bit of scrub over time - which is how forests start out - you will see fast growing plants like gorse, then birch and hazel seedlings will sprout, then probably holly. These 'pioneer plants' push out the grasses that have been living there. They also provide some shade, which is what acorns and ash-keys like.

The young oak and ash trees will grow straight upright and relatively close together: fast, because they are in competition for water and light, and close, because their parents are prolific seeders. They are seeking to reach sexual maturity to set more seed, not to get old, so they will race upwards.

A natural deciduous forest is full of tall but not very old and not very wide trees, whose natural lifespan is a lot shorter than when they are in fields and gardens, and they will cast dappled, but not dense, shade as a result. Under the trees So the plants of woodland - and this includes the huge range of rhododendrons and camellias - want the protection from hot sunshine and wind that a natural light forest will give, but cannot exist in dark shadow any more than any other plant. They like glades, rides and moisture.

In your own piece of woodland, or even under your single large-ish tree, the main flower show will be in spring up to about midsummer. If you can grow them, rhododendrons and azaleas will have their peak from about April into July. Lilies are largely woodland plants from China and the USA, and will give you colour about from June into August.

Green plants that actively like shade may be identified by large, thin leaves, to catch whatever light there is under trees, or their very dark colour: they have more chlorophyll, for the same reason. Hostas are classic plants of the Japanese woodland, although the fierce Japanese winters must kill off the slugs and snails that eat them here. Many ferns, but not all, enjoy shade.

Other woodlanders include hellebores, pulmonarias, heucheras, tiarellas and Gladdon iris (Iris foetidissima). There are some unexpected members of the saxifrage family, like London pride (Saxifraga x urbium) and Mother of Thousands (two similar plants are called this, Saxifraga stolonifera or Saxifraga fortunei).

The main woodland show in autumn will be hips and berries, plus whatever colour you get from autumn leaves. If you are on acid soil you will be able to grow maples, many of which turn bright yellow or red. If you have a lot of space, the more unusual plants like witch hazels (hamamelis) and parrotias may earn their keep - but not in a small garden.

On limey soil, birches are reliably yellow in autumn and cherry leaves usually turn red. Other leaf colours will depend a lot on how hot the summer has been as hotter summers tend to give brighter autumn leaves.

The great rhododendron gardens of the South and West are worth a visit. Note the extraordinary range of vivid colour in spring and often again in autumn, but also note that most are in enclosed dells or 'secret valleys', which deflect the wind. Many face south or west, to raise the temperature and cut out frost. These are also the only conditions where I would attempt the beautiful but expensive tree ferns from Tasmania as they need moisture all around them and protection from hot sun.

Digression: really big trees

Very big trees in the UK are usually there because a human being has planted them or protected them. People planted the huge chestnuts (sweet chestnuts were introduced by the Romans, horse chestnuts in about 1600), or plane trees (introduced about 1680) as none of these are native.

Very large oaks and yews have an ancient use as boundaries to fields or property, or to mark sacred space. Really old trees in the UK can be thousands of years old. Evergreens like holly and yew were favoured as these are markers all year round.

The word 'forest' is not about trees, in its origins. In geographical use, it still isn't; many upland areas named 'forests' in the north of England have hardly a tree.

The Norman French 'foret' is derived from the same word as 'foreign', so it's the place where foreigners i.e. Saxons, live. When deer parks and hunting parks like the New Forest were established for the Norman nobility in the eleventh century, the Saxon serfs who looked after them would protect some very big trees as boundaries and to provide shade for the deer-herds.

If you were a Saxon working in a foret, you had to mind your ways: you could commit crimes against the 'venison' (the animals in the reserve, which could only be hunted by the nobility) or the 'vert' (anything else). Trespasses against the vert included purpresture and assarting.

I'll save you the search; 'purpresture' is fencing off land that doesn't belong to you, and 'assarting' is clearing land by uprooting everything. Words we should bring back, I feel.

Head gardener's problems

You just can't get the servants these days.

Even wealthy households will now have a full-time garden staff counted on the fingers of one hand. The National Trust and the great public gardens like Kew depend on networks of volunteers and unpaid trainees. Times have changed.

Modern gardens look different, because they have to be. They may still be large. Beth Chatto's garden in Essex covers several acres, but little is in traditional herbaceous borders. One of my favourite gardens, Great Comp, is part woodland and part formal, but has very limited areas of traditional herbaceous or bedding plants.

The move to designing labour out of garden upkeep has been called 'low maintenance' gardening, but this should mean more than smothering the ground with fast growing but boring greenstuff, like a supermarket car-park.

Sustainability is also a watchword. Now that most of us pay for water on a meter, large-scale irrigation is becoming unaffordable. It is no longer socially acceptable to 'improve' your soil by covering it in large amounts of peat, to strip Lakeland hillsides to create your water-worn limestone patio, nor can you keep your delicate lovelies earwig-free by dousing them in poison.

Planting for reduced labour

To reduce your labour input, you need to plan cleverly and above all, work with the plant and your soil, not against them. If you don't want to grow weeds, make sure something else is growing there instead.

Ground-cover plants prevent weeds getting a grip because incomers are starved of light, water and space. A closely-knit planting of bergenia, herbaceous geranium, daylilies and arabis should need little weeding - once established. To get good coverage, you will need one big shrub or three to five large herbaceous plants per square metre. By large, I mean the size you see in garden centres, which are usually in 2 litre pots.

It is usually a false economy to use small plants as they take a lot longer to get established, which translates into more work looking after them. However, the new long borders at Kew were planted up with many plants in 9cm pots, and they look fine, so take your choice.

For shrubs, check what the mature width and height will be from the label. A small shrub like a hebe or a ground-cover rose will usually grow at least 60 cm across. Some, such as spreading junipers, get much wider. You should allow a big shrub like a mock orange (Philadelphus) at least one square metre per plant.

Arrange your pots or clumps so that everything has enough room to expand, then plant them. You can then cover the bed in shreddings, bark chips or gravel if you like. It will look spotty. Don't panic. And that should be that.

But in the first year, you will need to keep the area well-watered and the little weeds picked out, as the plants get their roots down into the soil.

You do not need fertiliser, because you have chosen your plants to suit the soil. You need to watch for bullying and overlaying, and you may choose to take off dead heads and cut plants back after flowering, but you may also choose not to.

Prairie and dry-soil (xeroscape) gardens

A more recent development has been so-called 'prairie' planting, spearheaded by designers like Piet Oudolf. There are two large borders at RHS Wisley in this style.

The idea is to use large clumps of a small number of types of vigorous plants, chosen carefully for the soil and conditions, so that they thrive without additional fertiliser or irrigation. These plants are then assembled in groups, which are repeated randomly over the area.

Prairie planting looks best from about July to October. Again, once established, this needs little looking after, apart from clearing dead stems in about March.

'Once established' is the key. Preparation of the soil is vital so if you don't want weeds poking through, then dig them out to start with. After that, if you are using shrubs you may want to consider putting down some dark landscape textile - you can get it from your garden centre - to stop weed seeds from germinating. To plant up your area, make cross-wise slits in the textile and put in your shrubs, then cover with bark mulch.

An extension of this idea is dry gardening. Again, there is a large example at Wisley just behind the new glasshouse, and there are impressive dry gardens at Beth Chatto's and at Hyde Hall. Dry gardening ('xeroscaping') uses naturally drought-resistant plants on sunny sandy, gravel or chalk soils.

Plants are placed across the bed or landscape, but not as close together as 'ground cover', because of the limited water available. Again, weeds find it hard to grow, this time because the established plants take all the water. If you finish this kind of bed with gravel, the extra heat reflecting from the stone may help your dry plants to flower more vigorously.

These styles of bed will need going-over a couple of times a year but, once planted, do not need extensive digging, hoeing, watering or feeding. They won't give you a Jekyll rainbow or a cottage garden explosion, but they should give several months of enjoyment.

Plants for prairie and dry-soil gardening

Prairie soils, as found in the Mid West of America or out in the great plains of Eastern Europe, are deep but light. They drain quickly, and because they are in the middle of a big land-mass, winters are cold and summers are hot. Prairies are flat and the wind cuts across them without interruption.

If you have a light, deep soil and sun in summer, prairie plants should do well. The main show will be from July to end October. Plants which have developed to cope with these conditions often have deep roots, to cope with summer drought, but are usually non-woody; you see few trees on a prairie. They grow away quickly in spring to take advantage of melting snow, but because they don't have time to grow a fleshy fruit, most depend on the wind to blow their seeds around.

Classic prairie plants include tall grasses, especially elephant grass (miscanthus) and varieties of (sorry, no common names, take a look at them at the garden centre) calamagrostis, stipa and pennisetum.

American prairie flowers include rudbeckia ('Black-eyed Susan'), echinacea (coneflower), coreopsis (tickseed), heleniums (sneezewort), eupatorium ('Queen of the Prairie') and tall Michaelmas daisies.

European 'prairies' will also grow Geranium pratense (cranesbills), tall centaureas (knapweeds), Verbascum bombiferum (Aaron's rod), tall achilleas (yarrow) and scabious.

You could also include the sea-holly Eryngium giganteum ('Miss Wilmott's Ghost') which will seed itself and gives a nice silvery effect. Ignore the name, it's not a giant, but about a metre tall.

Pick six or eight plants out of this list, or plants of similar height and requirements, balance them about forty percent grasses to sixty percent flowering plants, and then start putting them in repeating groups and drifts.

You might get away with some early spring bulbs like crocus, but later ones would be concealed by the height of the growing plants.

Plants for your desert

Deserts are marked by lack of rain, but also lack water-holding material in the soil. No humus has built up to hold water and slow evaporation. If you try hard you can turn almost any piece of land into a desert, as they don't have to be hot, only dry. A famous (small) area in Maine in the US was 'desertified' by bad farming practice, mainly overgrazing and failure to rotate crops.

Desertification in other parts of the world, like southern Spain, is driven by the removal of shelter of trees and shrubs, and over-ploughing soils which become light and broken, and blow away.

Once this has happened, there is nowhere for rain to go when it does fall. Water runs off in a flash flood or soaks straight through the sand and gravel that remain.

But there are also natural deserts and these contain some of the most brilliant flowering plants of all. The sudden bursts of flower in the Australian outback or the South African veldt are famous and astonishing.

Dry-soil plants include Yucca filamentosa (Adam's needle), South African daisies (Osteospermum, Venidio artctotis, Gerbera), and bulbs (nerines and gladioli).

In really hot dry areas like the centre of a town or a sheltered part of East Anglia, you may get away with aloes or desert yuccas ('Spaniards'). Many annuals come from desert areas, such as California poppies.

In the Mediterranean, dry hillsides (maquis) are covered with lavender, rosemary, cistus, oregano, euphorbias (spurges) such as Euphorbia wulfenii, and spiny acanthus. Crocus, tulips, salvias and golden or purple sages love these conditions, as do tall border irises.

The living garden

Bees and other citizens of your garden

In my childhood, I could lie on my back in a recreation ground field, and hear the hum of the bees and the chirp of the crickets. I would also see more than one butterfly.

If you want your children to have that experience, you can do something about it. I'll leave all the arguments about farmers needing pollinators and disruption of the ecology – you can find those elsewhere. This is about what gardens can contribute.

Bees and butterflies and pollinators need nectar. This is made of water and sugars, and insects use it as an energy food. Pollen – the yellow dust in the middle of the flower – is protein, and insects eat it to make eggs or feed new butterflies, bees and other insects. Both come from – and only from – flowers.

The creatures in your neighbourhood are not actually that picky. While some butterfly caterpillars will only feed on one group of plants, nectar-feeders don't care much, but they do like a well-appointed buffet.

The studies showing that 'native' wild areas are preferred by bees may well be because the density of food (nectar and pollen) is much higher in a wild area than a well-weeded border 'n' lawn garden.

So, which flowers 'work' for bees and butterflies? If flowers have nectar, most will, but there need to be lots of them, and as many bees now emerge early (Christmas, sometimes, for the big bumblebees) they need to be available for as long as possible.

My personal observations of favoured 'bee plants' are as follows:
Spring:
Heather.
Primroses and primulas.
Pulmonaria (lungwort)
Comfrey, tall or low (Symphytum 'Hidcote Blue').
Spot the hairy-footed flower bee.

Early summer:
Apple and other fruit blossom.
Single roses: my Rosa moyesii got so full of bumble-bees, it was a singing, ringing tree.
Honey garlic (Nectaroscordum).
Bluebells.
Rosemary.
Foxgloves (bumble bees fight over them).

Broad bean flowers.

High summer:

Thistly flowers like artichokes, globe thistles (Echinops), and sea holly (Eryngium).

Knapweeds and cornflowers (Centaurea).

Big open daisies like marguerites.

Marjoram.

'Platform' shaped flowers like Ammi, fennel or Achillea.

Very important: 'lipped' flowers (labiates) like snapdragons, sage, ornamental salvias (bush or bedding), lavender, germander, thyme, lamb's ear and mint.

And, of course, clover.

See the wool-carder bee, a feisty insect that collects 'wool' from silver-leafed plants for its nest, and can hover or fly backwards like a Harrier jet.

Painted lady butterflies love red valerian, and plenty of others adore buddleia.

Watch the leaf-cutter bee painstakingly trim a coin-sized piece out of young rose leaves – and leave her to it. The plant will recover.

Autumn, into winter:

Wherever insects can spot the nectar and pollen. Highly double flowers don't count, no matter how scented.

Tall sedums, like 'Autumn Joy' or 'Matrona'.

Ivy – the flowers are the black or green knobby bits, also seen on fatsia and fatshedera.

Snowberry flowers.

Mahonia.

And caterpillars need -
Nettles, honesty, vetch, charlock, rape
Rocket, privet, garlic mustard,
violets, primroses Holly, ivy, sorrel, and long grass.
You get the picture. If you want butterflies, don't be too tidy.

Now, the lawn. The biggest potential unused refuge of them all.

If your garden is hard landscape, close-mown lawn and conifers, this might as well be the Sahara for insects. So lay out the buffet, and learn to love a 'shag-pile' effect, with lots of little flowers (clover, daisies, buttercups, ladies' fingers, self-heal).

Cut high and only when absolutely needed, not just because it's Sunday. Call it a 'flowery mead', if you like, as seen in Botticelli's Primavera. And put away the weedkillers, the paving and the concrete. Bees need flowers.

Organics: killing the eco-friendly way

I will leave the moral arguments for the organic approach to those who are more comfortable with them, and examine what is meant by organic gardening - because this does not necessarily mean gardening without chemicals, nor gardening without killing.

The founders of the modern organic movement included Laurence Hills and Henry Doubleday, who were active in the nineteen-twenties and thirties. They were convinced, as were those in the naturism, herbalism and vegetarian movements of the time, that modern man suffered from being divorced from nature, and that over-processing of food and over-reliance on 'unnatural' practices such as the use of chemical fertilisers was poisoning human society.

A lot of 'muck and mystery' has been attached to the movement since, unfortunately. The contribution by the flower-power generation of the Sixties has not exactly clarified matters.

An organic approach has a lot of good points. The basic underlying scientific philosophy (and there is a lot of hard-science research into organic gardening and farming) is to work with nature, with the soil and the natural propensities of plants.

Wherever possible, plants are encouraged to defend themselves from disease, by growing strong and so tough that they grow through challenges. Pests can be kept at bay by other means than poisoning them, such as putting cages over vegetable and fruit plots, and barriers around carrots and over the soil around strawberries. The Soil Association is the guardian of thinking on organic growing in the UK, and has a website and publications.

The general idea is that better the soil, the faster a plant will grow, and the more chance of reaching flower or harvest before the pests notice and strip it to a twig. Most of the time.

Pests and problems: get ready to squish

There are some problems that the organic approach has yet to conquer. Slugs and snails are one. There are 'organic' slug-killers around, but they are not as effective as the blue metaldehyde pellets, now banned. Wool pellets are a new idea that may provide a physical barrier.

Many 'sharp' remedies are useless, as slugs and snails can crawl over a razor blade without harm if they wish. They do, however, respond to the mild electrical charge in a strip of copper tape, if this is put around the rim of a pot. Remember, though, that they can crawl from leaf to leaf - a friend thinks they abseil - so keep your pots well apart.

Caterpillars are another problem. Some moths tend to have population explosions every few years. Some, such as the tortrix moths and gooseberry sawfly, can quite easily kill a shrub.

You can pick them all off by hand or you can spray. Organic sprays only kill the insects they land on, they do not give any continuing protection.

Fungal diseases like mildew are another problem area. The 'organic' fungicides are highly toxic, based on sulphur and copper salts, and again these deliver no protective benefits.

Some so-called biological controls have been marketed as organic on the doubtful premise that it is morally better to kill slugs by infecting them with hundreds of tiny parasitic worms rather than knock them out with poison.

Biological controls work. Kew Gardens, Wisley and most commercial glasshouse growers use them, because they are highly efficient. But they are still killers.

What's in your spray

Bugs such as leather jackets, chafers, lily beetles, vine weevils, flea beetles, cabbage white caterpillars and other critters may make your gardening life difficult. If you can see a manageable number, you can squash them by hand. Otherwise, you have a choice between organic contact sprays, or chemically-produced ones.

Most organic sprays are made from types of rotenone and pyrethrin, both insecticides obtained from plants and dissolved in detergent. Their main advantage, apart from leaving no active chemicals in the soil, is that edible crops are ready for picking within a day of use.

Like any contact insecticide, they kill what they land on, including bees, so care is needed in their use.

Insecticides that are based on advanced chemicals can be slightly more selective, and can also be taken up systemically into the plant's 'bloodstream' for longer-term protection. Some are of very long pedigree, while others are modern creations. Any that are on sale to gardeners have passed human toxicity tests although most are still extremely poisonous.

The basic rule is that all insecticides and fungicides, whether 'organic' or not, are poisonous, and some are very dangerous. 'Organic' copper sulphate mixes can be as fatal as the now-banned 'inorganic' paraquat.

Treat them all with care, always make sure they are correctly labelled, never leave them where children or pets can get to them and use them all as sparingly as you can.

Bigger pests, such as squirrels, rabbits, pigeons and the neighbour's cat, are trickier to deal with. For fruit and vegetable areas, netting or a permanent cage structure are good, albeit expensive, solutions. It takes a good few years of home-grown vegetables to pay back the cost of even a small ready-built structure.

For the ornamental garden, this is not an option, although in areas where rabbits or deer are a pest, perimeter fencing may be worth considering. Otherwise you are back to low-tech silver paper strips on black cotton. That, and throwing wellies.

Further musings

Dinosaur diets

What, you may ask in an idle moment, did dinosaurs eat? Apart from other dinosaurs? Well, as they went extinct 65 million years ago, the answer is, mainly plants that do not have flowers, such as ferns, mosses, cycads, gingko and conifers.

But flowering plants began to evolve 60 million years earlier, so nuts or fruits did exist. The first flowering plants were probably water-plants and not very impressive, but what we gardeners would call flowers started appearing about 130 million years ago, during the Cretaceous. This is also when flowering plants split into two main groups. Note that there were no bees - yet. Primitive flowers used beetles as pollinators.

One-quarter of all flowering plant species are 'monocots', including orchids, grasses, palms, and aroids (arum lily family) but also lilies, daffodils and ginger. You will see, if you grow them from seed, that when they start growing they put up only one (mono) grass-like seed leaf (cotyledon) - so mono-cot. Other plants, like beans, have two seed-leaves, so are called dicots.

Ancient plant groups from before the time of the split between types, about 100 million years ago, include peperomias (which you may grow as a house plant) and the climber that produces black pepper.

So dinosaurs could have eaten primitive palms and pepper but not grasses or bamboo, which only evolved about 40 million years ago.

Palms may be a tough ask in the UK but we can grow the Chusan plan, Trachycarpus fortunei, and some in the south can get away with fan palms like Washingtonia. Other 'dinosaur trees' are the gingko – which is much, much older than the dinosaurs but can be slow to grow in the UK – and some types of conifer, notably monkey-puzzle trees and their relative, the Wollemi pine.

Underneath the monkey-puzzles, dinosaurs could graze on cycads - again, just about possible outdoors in the southern UK – but also on ferns. Here we have a wide choice even today, but most can't stand much sun.

Ferns to grow as a carpet include oak and beech ferns - look for Polypodium, Polystichum and Dryopteris - as well as the bog-lovers like Osmunda. The maidenhair ferns, Adiantum, are rare natives and need somewhere shady and damp, such as beside a Welsh waterfall. Harts-tongue ferns, Asplenium, are much tougher and may be found on drystone walls, and others in the asplenium group can also stand drier conditions.

Tree ferns are dramatic but need attention, and don't stand frost very well. Bracken is a pest and poisonous to cattle and horses.

Magnolias are so old, they show features of both monocots and dicots. They are one of the oldest flowering plant groups, traceable in fossils 95 million years old, and they have not changed a lot since. Dinosaurs could have browsed beneath their branches.

Magnolias' resemblance to waterlilies - also a very ancient group - reflects a basic primitive flower design. Today, magnolias grow wild in Asia, especially southern China and Indonesia, and in the south-eastern USA down into Latin America. Most prefer acid soil and a warm climate.

In the UK we get away with some of the tougher Chinese magnolias. If, as in recent years, we have a 'green' winter, the display can be extraordinary. The big pink and purple ones are Magnolia soulangiana or Magnolia liliflora, the white or pink ones with smaller starry flowers are Magnolia stellata, and really big white ones are probably 'yulan' types.

The huge evergreen one flowering in midsummer is Magnolia grandiflora, called the 'bull bay' in its Louisiana home. In a really hot year, magnolias may set seed in rather peculiar red, sausage-like structures. (In a frosty year, all you'll get is a heap of soggy brown petals).

Many dramatic magnolias can take many years to mature enough to flower. The really big types like the waterlily tree, Magnolia campbelli, and Magnolia grandiflora, may keep you waiting for 50 years. The big trees in front gardens are possibly flowering so well now because they were planted in the 1950's or before.

However, new varieties are bred for early maturity, so be sure to look at the label. Look out for 'Exmouth', 'Susan', 'Betty', 'Rustica Rubra' or 'Leonard Messel'. Many are now bred in Canada and New Zealand, so there's no problem with toughness.

Some of the best specimen magnolias in Sussex are at Wakehurst Place and Nymans, where you can see exotics like Magnolia macrophylla, which likes growing underneath big trees. Some less usual American species like Magnolia virginiana (sweetbay) typically flower in July and August. Most are sweetly scented, with sweetbay and bull bay especially so, like lemon sherbet.

With recent mild winters, flower buds will start to be obvious in March. Squirrels can be a pest if they take a fancy to the buds. So remember to let your velociraptor loose, for the full Cretaceous effect.

A Spot of Science

My musings on magnolias set me thinking about the scientific oddities of plants. A lot of people tend to treat them like green pets, especially house-plants, but, it may seem obvious to say, plants are not animals. (Pause while everyone rakes through distant, long-lost memories of biology lessons on photosynthesis). Plants differ in chemistry, geometry - Spectacles on, everyone.

First, **chemistry**. Plants obtain energy and make tissue from sunlight and carbon dioxide, but the green structures inside plant cells that do this, the chloroplasts, were once independent algae, which were enveloped into the cells as symbiotes. Photosynthesis is a highly complex process; you can read Brian Cox on the energy gradient, or Jim Al Khalili on the quantum physics aspects. Plants may use not one but three different chemical routes.

Most plants are classified as 'C3' but about 3% of plants, often tropical and including important crops like maize, use the 'C4' route, possibly an adaptation to tougher growing conditions. CAM plants, often desert species, are about 6% of known plants, and use a system involving malic acid. That's one for the pub quiz.

Geometry: If you're a plant, the best way to arrange your leaves for maximum light comes down to mathematics. A dome is good shape as each leaf gets sun as it passes overhead and does not shade others out. Or you can grow upwards, side by side, to the same height as all the others.

If you stretch a dome upwards, to get sideways light as well, you get a cone. You can also raise your dome off the ground and above the competition, on a trunk. Motility: plants inevitably point towards the best source of light. But they cannot move, so this is achieved by selective cell death and growth.

So if you plant a conical tree where half is in permanent shade, that half will die off, and the plant will grow towards the light. No amount of pruning will alter this. And if you prune it into a shape that is - for the plant - a very inefficient trap for light, don't be surprised if its natural instinctive shape re-emerges.

Society: Plants take in some additional nutrients from the soil through their roots, but only as a liquid solution.

We now know that many, perhaps most, plants use tiny fungi, the mycorrhizae which live on the surface of roots, to predigest nutrients. Again, this is a symbiotic relationship. Only plants that live on acid soils, like rhododendrons, lack mycorrhizae.

But perhaps plants' least animal-like feature is **genetic**. If you or I, or any animal, lack a chromosome or have an extra one, this is can be disastrous. Plants can be stuffed with chromosomes and it does not seem to matter. Animals have a pair of identical sets of chromosomes, called the 'diploid' number, but plants can have three (triploid), four (tetraploid) up to - almost unbelievably - a thousand, in a primitive fern called the adder's tongue. Adding chromosome sets makes the cell bigger, and is one way of increasing plant size.

It also means less-related plant species can be crossed. If plant A is triploid (3 sets) and plant B is tetra (4 sets) then if you quadruple the set count in A and triple it in B, you get plants with 12 sets that can be crossed. The multiple chromosome sets can be created by chemicals such as colchicine.

And if you get extra marks in your local pub quiz for any of that, just save me a pint.

My gardens

In my gardening life, I have owned five gardens and been heavily involved in three others, owned by family members, over a long period. They were/are all 'work in progress'.

I should also emphasise that I am not a gardener or garden designer by profession. I buy my own materials and I have to live with my mistakes.

I have been a member of the RHS for – ooh, ever such a long time (1981 – I've just checked). When I first joined, I think they had 40,000 members. I believe it's heading to 500,000 these days, which possibly explains why the parking at Wisley is so congested at weekends.

I am also an active supporter of Kew Gardens, especially their conservation programme in Madagascar.

My gardens are spaces for me and my friends, and have not been open to the public, but are expected to be pleasant and entertaining all year.

Garden One

My first gardening memory is planting little purple violas when I was about four, but I know I first went to Kew at age two, my (big, old, copper) penny in my hand, and I've been going ever since. The first garden I owned was attached to a very small Victorian terraced house and was ten feet wide by about thirty feet long (3m by 9m).

The soil was hugely rich, which I now realise was because it had been the recipient of many, many chamber-pots over the years. When I planted my 'children's mixture', the cornflowers leapt up to 4 feet/1.2 m without even trying. However, as the garden was so limited in space, and I was learning, it did not have an interesting layout. These days I would put up trellis panels to about 5 feet/1.4 m and use a Mondrian-style plan.

But inevitably in a tiny garden adjoined by others on all sides, the opportunities for a private space are not good, unless you are prepared to put up with a lot of shade. I had that garden for three years, by which time I was convinced that this was my hobby for life. So I wanted a bigger one –

Garden Two

This was rather larger, behind a semi-detached house, at 60 feet/20m long by about twenty-five feet/ 8m at the widest part – in other words, behind the garage. There was a greenhouse, a terrace, and full height fencing and walls all round, of pierced blocks. The soil was not great, being gravelly.

Because the garden faced south, it could bake solid. This is when I discovered that a south-facing terrace could become unusably hot in the summer months even in the UK. The greenhouse allowed me to grow tomatoes reasonably well, but also pots of chrysanthemums - if you want a plant for autumn show and to cut for the house, give spray chrysanthemums a go.

I tried roses and fuchsias and herbaceous plants and bulbs and alpines. I had a very impressive Asarina procumbens, a spreading plant from Spain, which loved the heat, and I released two forsythias from hedgehoggery by not pruning them into a blob. But I wanted more space.

Garden Three

I had this garden for thirty years. The plot was about 100 feet/30 metres long at the back, with a small north-facing paved area about 4m / 12 feet square and a conservatory at the rear of the house. At the front, the south-facing garden was about 30 feet/10 m deep, giving on to a relatively busy road. The plot was 30 feet/10m wide, but a section of the garden at the rear was taken out because of the garage.

The soil is heavy yellow river clay. It was heavy clay when I moved in, and it will be to the End of Days. That's how I know it's unimprovable.

I spent a lot of time trying things out to see what will grow in what is basically uncooked London brick. Roses can be iffy and prairie daisies don't like it much at all.

The first thing I did was – measure it all up, mapped the garden and decided to divide the space roughly into four.

1. The terrace, for pots of things that like shade or acid soil
2. A point half-way down the lawn, which would become the division for the 'upper garden'
3. The garden below that, or 'lower garden'
4. A section created by extending a line from the side of the garage to the half-way point, which was to be the utility and kitchen garden.

I decided I needed some additional height at the half-way point, so I planted the (then tiny, eventually 15m) Eucalyptus dalrympleana.

I also, with help from my dad, placed some upright posts and a post going across in a sort of half-pergola, up which to grow climbers and visually divide the garden. I put smaller posts in around the kitchen garden, added wires and planted a vine and a fern-leafed blackberry - then wished I hadn't. It produced far too many thorny babies.

My first choices of shrubs were Rosa moyesii, which grew 4 metres high and across, an amelanchier for spring blossom, a big orange blossom and a kerria. The kerria died, the orange blossom got to 4 metres.

Over the years some roses survived but many modern roses did not, so here's a shout out for 'Bloomfield Abundance' and 'Perle d'Or', which are troupers. Herbaceous geraniums did well, like 'Mrs Kendall Clark', 'Walney', 'Rozanne', as did black bamboo and golden bamboo, honey garlic (Nectaroscordum) a fig tree and a Chusan palm.

After the usual deaths and disasters I decided to widen the borders, which ended up the length of the garden on the left side, averaging 4 feet/1.2 m wide, getting wider under the 'pergola'. On the right, after a utility space, the bed curved but averaged 3 feet/1 m wide. At the bottom was a pond, a wild area under an oak, about 10 feet/3 m deep, plus two oval beds.

The pergola finally died in the windy winter of 2013, leaving the white rose 'Mme Albert Carriere' as a small tree. I had an 'ivy tree' where the remaining post supported a large variegated ivy bush 3 m high by 2 m across, until another wind took it in 2016.

After years of growing poor and very expensive veg, the 'kitchen garden' was reborn as a 'secret garden' with a bench, roses, and space for exotic bedding.

Garden Four

In 2013 I decided to invest in a weekend home, which also had a garden, on the south coast. The sunlight is far better than London although temperatures are cooler and there is a coastal wind. The garden was flat, 25 m long by 12 m wide (82 feet by 40 feet). The soil is light clay. This is about a kilometre from the sea as the gull flies.

The site faces south but is shaded by big trees on a boundary. I had it landscaped (see what I did there? Someone else swung the pickaxe on this one) resulting in three sections:

1 an existing paved area at the bottom with a shed

2 a gravelled area for the outdoor dining set

3 nearest the house, a D-shaped lawn surrounded by relatively deep flower beds, which were rotavated.

Most of the old garden was grass, with few plants apart from some large buddleias, a snowball tree, a golden bamboo, and a Pseudacacia 'Frisia'.

Things That Should Have Done Well by 2018, But Didn't

•Lavender: 2 lost (unknown variety), no particular reason. French lavender (Lavandula stoechas) and 'Munstead' managed two years, just. Not a plant for open soil even here.

•Convolvulus cneorum: Two lost over winter, root-rot. These are bright, bright silver, favourites of mine but need a sharply drained soil like gravel or sand.

•Purple sage: see lavender. One lost, two growing like stink. Who knows why.

•Rudbeckia 'Goldsturm': Very iffy, hanging on but not thriving. Soil too heavy? Later went altogether.

Things That Surprised Me

•Self-seeded Italian camomile (Anthemis cupaniana) – luckily I'm fond of it. Later discovered it probably blew in off the shingle spit at Pagham.

• Kerria japonica (orange flowers in spring) spread out and tied against a fence. This worked well, mass of bloom and green leaves followed, but the wet winter of 2019 killed it.

•Pony Tails grass (Stipa tenuissima), an 'accident' from my sister's, spreading and bulking up well.

•Mirabilis jalapa, the four o'clock plant. Tubers like a dahlia, survived the clearance. Grows to 60 cm or so, white, red or yellow flowers in late summer.

Things That Did Far, Far Better Than Expected

•Rose 'Valentine Heart' – grows like a cabbage, flowers May to October. Ditto 'Birthday Girl' and 'You're Beautiful'.

•A special mention for beautifully scented rose 'Natasha Richardson'.

•Rosa banksia lutea is huge in only 3 years.

•Lamb's Lugs (Stachys lanata or byzantina): I could supply West Sussex.

•Catmint (Nepeta 'Six Hills Giant') trebled in size.

•Geranium 'Sweet Heidi'. An ever-expanding patch over a metre across, dies down in winter.

•Kniphofias (Red Hot Pokers) all growing their socks off. Later removed because the leaf to flower ratio was not good enough for me, but retained 'Toffee Nose' and 'Pineapple Popsicle', and caulescens (species).

•Lemon Verbena (Aloysia citrodora) now a bush 1.5 metres high and across, next to a hot patio area.

•Fern-leaved elder (Sambucus) came in by pigeon, grew to over 3 metres in 3 years.

Things that Got the Chop Early

•Lavatera is a useful plant for big pink flowers in June, but it SPREADS. Mine was 2 metres high and across in 2 years, but was knocked flat by wind and overlaid other things. So out it came.

•Bedding osteospermums did not take, and a wet July/August did for them.

Overall, a learning experience, as well as a source of cuttings for my next garden.

Garden Five

This is my 'new garden' about eight miles from Number Four, originally laid out in the early seventies but not much changed since.

Some of the shrubs had become Octopussy monsters. You can be unexpectedly savage when pruning some 1970's favourites: cherry laurel can be cut back to its toes as can Portugal laurel and yew. Leyland cypresses cannot, and will not grow away after pruning dead stuff out. If they're big and half dead, that's as good as they will ever be. Down they come.

Right. Now had ENORMOUS heap of cherry laurel, spotted laurel, dead kerria, overgrown/dead choisya, spindly old lilac, a mattress of old clematis montana and stuff off a birch tree. All ready to be cut into bits to fit in the car and taken to the dump or stuffed in the green bin.

Found a chap to cut the lawn and do the heavy tree work so MUCH happier now. In the end, he also took two cart-loads of stuff away, which was money well spent.

The roses were of unknown age, so I pruned them to see a) if they survive and b) how pretty they are. One turns out to be 'Golden Showers', a good climber, but the others I have not identified. Several are small, delicate single flowered bush or patio roses in crimson, and two are very pretty but dainty cream/white with a small pink edge. I am preserving them.

But the most useful thing you can do in a new garden is put down the secateurs, bring out a garden chair, and sit in various parts of the garden at different times of day. This shows the variations in light, temperature, wind and viewpoint. If you're keen and think you may have more than one type of soil, dig a little test pit.

After 'consulting the genius of the place', as poet Alexander Pope put it (a very keen gardener), start to allocate where you will do or grow what.

Kitchen and herb gardens need to be near the kitchen. If your garden is big enough, which this one is, have a sunny sitting area, but also a shady one. The bottom of the garden needs a purpose or it will simply become an unvisited dumping ground. This is your opportunity for your hobby cabin, 'home pub', a secret sitting area, or a 'different' garden (sculpture, Japanese, pond, gnomes - up to you).

Mine was immediately christened Dingly Dell by my sister but I prefer Shady Nook. It had the world's biggest heap of dead leaves but is now cleared out ready to become a separate seating area under the trees, with shade planting. Also a good place to keep cuttings and seedlings.

So far, I have identified sites for a sunny flower border, a shaded border, a Mediterranean terrace, a woodland bit and the Nook. I don't have acres so these are not necessarily very big.

I need to find somewhere for a new shed but I won't be doing much hard landscaping. I really don't like using more concrete than I absolutely have to. And I certainly won't be doing it all at once, or on my own.

But I will get turf lifted and the shed in place, and get the 'bones' ready for planting. And hope that, despite being in an archaeological hotspot, I don't find any real bones. Archaeologists can be rather messy.

Your master checklist

That's it. You now understand your garden, you've got an idea about colours, tastes and styles, what you're going to do, and how to achieve your effect. Let's put it all together.

1. Your garden plot
Size
Shape
Aspect (north, south, east or west-facing)
Soil type
Permanent features
How many areas or sections

2. Practical requirements
Water
Access
Boundary markers
Power
Storage
Shelter
Privacy
Entertaining
Wildlife
Main areas by usage
For each member of the family or potential user, where are his or her areas of use. Are they happy with these? (So ask them. Shared spaces are inevitably compromise spaces).

3 Mood and style
For each section of garden, what is the desired mood?
What is the desired style?
What boundary is there between one section and the next, to create mystery or a 'journey'?
How much time can you give for upkeep on a weekly basis in spring and summer
What is your on-going budget for each section of garden?
Will you be growing your own bedding and tender plants or buying them in.

4 Plants
Have you included your favourite plants?
Have you included your favourite colours?
Have you included enough height?
Have you got enough evergreens?
Have you been restrained with variegated foliage?
Will there be something to look at in all seasons

Are the hard landscaping, walls, painted areas, furniture etc. going to harmonise with the colour scheme for the plants

5 Your vista:

What will you see easily, along each major line of sight (not 'I know it's there because I planted it')

The major lines of sight are straight down the garden, from side to side at the mid-point, and the two lines to the far left and far right corners from your main viewpoint. Think Union Jack.

And does this hide or reveal stuff you don't want to see, like bins or your neighbour's bathroom window?

What are the views in
Spring
Summer
Autumn
Winter

6 What is /will be your favourite place in the garden and why, in
Spring
Summer
Autumn
Winter

7 Does the garden as you have now planned it, meet the needs as you listed them to start with?

If not, have you changed ideas – or have you gone off-course?

This is your space. There is an argument that, in most forms of artistic expression, you do it, then you go back and do it again, but this time how you really meant it to be.

In planning a garden, it is easy to be swayed by fashion, or the latest TV programme, or what seems to be 'good taste' or what next door have done. But if this is to be a garden for you and everyone who shares your space, don't be afraid to be different.

To make the most of your garden, you need to be in it. That means the space has to be fun, useful and inviting for you. Not the style police next door, your mother in law or some nosy garden writer like me. So off you go, brave garden explorer –

.

Societies

Every area has at least one local horticultural society, Britain in Bloom committee or allotments group, and these can be very helpful to the beginner, but you can learn to garden using books, TV and YouTube as well.

The big national society is the RHS, which runs five show gardens across the country, and big flower shows through the year. As a member you get a monthly magazine, free or discounted entry to a lot of gardens and shows, and access to scientific advice and a comprehensive website.

There are a range of specialist societies, for example for roses, alpine plants, or rhododendrons, and if you want to get further into botany, the bigger botanical gardens offer memberships.

If you want to train or study further, the RHS oversees a comprehensive series of horticultural exams which are usually attached to a local horticultural or agricultural college, or may be run from a large garden centre or nursery.

You can get professional diploma qualifications through FE colleges, and some professional bodies also offer their own courses, such as the Landscape Institute.

Websites

Websites do change quite fast, so I would recommend doing your own free search. There are a lot of sites in the US, but be aware that UK growing conditions are a lot different and the rules on chemicals and environmental law are different as well.

The RHS free to access website contains guides to plant selection, lists of nurseries by area and seasonal/problem pages as well.

DEFRA is the source for official UK guidance on pests, diseases, and permitted works in gardens. YouTube is invaluable for watching someone take a cutting or doing something fiddly, but - general warning about the Net - there are no editors on free-access channels, so be aware that not all the advice may be tried and tested.

Garden visiting

The NGS ('Yellow Book')

If you know little about gardens or are new to the area, the National Garden Scheme Yellow Book system has to be the best way to see domestic gardening in action. The NGS operates 'open gardens' across the UK.

Garden owners compete to be listed in the 'Yellow Book', also available in an on-line version. Gardens listed will open on one or more days in the year. Gardens are selected on the basis that they offer at least 40 minutes of interest to a visitor, although the guidelines are elastic for very small but interesting gardens and some are only backyards.

The judging standards are high. Some large gardens are included, such as National Trust and English Heritage properties, but the majority are privately owned and less than country estates. This is the best way to find out what grows near you.

Go on to the website, ask for a list of gardens within a short travelling distance – say 10 miles – and on Sundays and some weekdays during spring and summer, there will be a choice of local gardens to visit. Fewer are open in autumn but there are late and early season gardens as well.

You will pay to enter but proceeds go to charity. Many gardens offer tea and cake (a bit of a highlight, actually) and some offer plants for sale, although you have to get there early to nab these.

'Open Gardens' are usually well signposted with distinctive yellow 'arrow' signs although you have to check about parking. Big gardens may have their own parking but semi-detached houses won't, so check on the site or in the book.

The National Trust

This is the guardian of many great houses and their associated grounds and gardens, as well as large chunks of coastline, natural woodland and habitats, of course. The Trust manages two of the most famous gardens in the world, Stowe and Sissinghurst, and a long list of the most influential gardens in the country, such as Biddulph Grange, Hidcote, Tatton Park, Stourhead, Packwood House and Anglesey Abbey. Pity the managers who have to plan for (and budget for) everything from the Victorian follies of Biddulph Grange to the massive landscape of Stowe, let alone the showcase that is Sissinghurst.

The National Trust does not get everything right. Some of their gardens were beginning to get a rather institutional look but there seems to have been some devolution recently, allowing more personality into planning, and a move away from 'deadly good taste', which is the danger for any garden designed by committee.

The National Trust also has to choose between preservation, conservation and evolution. Gardens do not stand still, but for visitors who have come to see a centuries-old famous view, or to see the photographs in reality, there is a risk of disappointment. So not everything may be leaf-perfect when you visit. The real question for the National Trust is whether they guard the spirit of a place, not every rhododendron in it.

English Heritage

I suspect they ended up in the gardens business rather by accident. EH were originally the Ancient Monuments people, which meant land management was about keeping the grass down to a reasonable level around castles and standing stones, and maintaining footpaths.

However, English Heritage also manage some large estates such as Audley End, Chiswick House, Brodsworth, Burton Agnes Hall and Witley Court, all of which have major historic gardens attached.

In recent years, English Heritage have led the way in getting modern garden-designers to provide settings for major visitor sites such as Eltham Palace and Walmer Castle. I suspect they saw how popular garden visiting has become, and that this could encourage people to revisit their sites for pleasure as well as education. So definitely worth a look.

English Heritage have a website and a handbook, and there is a membership scheme.

Kew Gardens

One of the great botanic gardens and research establishments in the world, not only the UK, Kew started out as a royal palace and hunting reserve. It was 'improved' in the eighteenth century under the influence of Princess Augusta, daughter-in-law of George the Second, to receive examples of the newly fashionable science of botany from around the world.

In its 250-plus years, Kew has built glasshouses, laboratories, lakes, a pagoda, temples, libraries and a herbarium, and has opened restaurants, shops, children's play areas, an art gallery and a small garden centre. You can admire its vast compost heap, too.

Kew leads ecological restoration in places such as Madagascar, and is responsible for the Millennium Seed Bank, containing a globally-important collection of seeds kept ready for germination at its Sussex location at Wakehurst. The gardens are now designed for show as well as science, and make a good day out.

Local authority, college and university gardens

Many of the great public parks designed by the Victorians have flower gardens and conservatories at their centre, which are now being appreciated and restored to former glories.

These are notable in Glasgow, Salford, Liverpool, Leeds (which has its own Rain Forest) and many other major cities, as well as the new National Garden in Wales. All are worth a visit and most are free. Horticultural colleges will often have show gardens attached, open for a small fee.

Older universities often have botanic gardens. They are of international standard in Oxford and Cambridge, both founded for the study of medicinal and 'economic' plants in the seventeenth century, but now designed for show as well as science.

Private estates

Oddly enough, not every major house or garden is in the hands of the National Trust. Some families have kept their money and their estates together by managing not to have a Fourth Earl who spent it all on the gaming tables of Monaco and ran off with the housekeeper.

These include some of the most magnificent country houses in England such as Chatsworth, Blenheim, Althorp, Alnwick Castle and Castle Howard, but also a wide range of houses and castles on a smaller scale.

In the south see Lullingstone Castle, now with Tom Hart-Dyke's World Garden attached, Groombridge Place, Hever Castle, Parham House, Arundel Castle and Penshurst Place. Most aristocratic families seem to have produced at least one manic gardener, so many estates have interesting historic gardens and grounds.

Today (as for English Heritage) many families have also decided to 'leverage' the attraction of the house by using the asset in which it stands, the land. Unconstrained by public committees and preservation, this has meant the freedom (if they wish) to install modern gardens and planting, hidden gardens, secret gardens and play gardens.

The multi-million pound construction of the gardens at Alnwick Castle is being driven by one person, the current Duchess of Northumberland. But then, most major gardens are the product of one dream and one vision.

Gardener's gardens

Every great private garden reaches a moment of truth when the gardener dies, or chooses to withdraw from managing the garden. The question then is, what to do next. In some families, a garden may be passed down generations. There have been three generations of female gardeners at Hatfield House, for example. The pre-marriage interview must be interesting ('Do you love my son, and can you prune a wisteria?').

But in gardens with a single guiding hand, as at Sissinghurst or Great Dixter, this may not be possible. In some cases, the answer has been to set up a charitable trust, to keep the gardens operational. This is been done at Great Dixter, Lambrook Manor, the Dorothy Clive Garden, Denmans, the Gibberd Garden near Harlow, and several others.

The key is to find a new head gardener who will maintain the outlines and spirit of the garden without being afraid to change. Great Dixter has been lucky in Fergus Garrett, who worked beside Christopher Lloyd for many years, and Great Comp has found new managers in the Dyson Nursery, who are keeping Roddy Cameron's vision alive.

So when you visit a 'famous' garden, don't expect to find it the way the famous gardener left it twenty years ago. Gardens are a sequence of fleeting visions, where the individual elements will never be the same from season to season, let alone year to year. But in the best, the overall vision should be maintained.

The perils of photography

When recommending books, I find that many of my favourites have no photographs. The experience-dense, fact-based accounts of garden development or descriptions of plants in major reference books are usually rather light on illustration.

In the past this was partly because producing books with coloured photo pages was expensive and glossy paper makes the books very heavy. The really big ones, the 'coffee table books', do require their own permanent position to have any hope of being read at all.

But today's print techniques permit illustrations within text, and then there's the internet, where a photo has no 'cost' or weight at all. But what does a photo add? You might think 'it tells you what the plant looks like' but that is only true up to a point.

It shows you want 'That' plant looked like at 'That' moment when framed up by 'That' photographer in 'That' light. And the selection of plant, moment and light has been manipulated to give the best possible image. Will the plant look the same in your garden? Maybe - but maybe not.

There is a fashion for very high magnification shots, which show internal structures or colours which you might not otherwise notice, but unless you usually assess your garden from a distance of fifteen centimetres/six inches, they are not a very good guide for garden use.

The things you need to know about a plant before you buy it or plant it, are facts like height when mature, width when mature, how long does 'mature' take, is it evergreen, what colour are the flowers or berries, how big are they, how long does it flower for, do you get a lot of flowers or just a few big ones, and does it have any special needs to grow well (like acid soil, sun or no sun, can it stand up to winds etc).

The very best way to judge a plant is to see it growing, which is why garden and park visiting is such a good idea. Take a photo if you like for reference, but that's only part of the process. That boring old textbook comes in next, which is crammed with information in a way that the internet cannot manage.

If you want a book of plants with reference shots, I can thoroughly recommend the series by Roger Phillips and Martyn Rix, which show the whole plant or flower in a comparative way, and usually a shot of the plant in its natural setting. But you will still need that text-book. I take reference shots to remind me of particular points, but I appreciate gardens by being there.

A garden is not a single moment reproduced in 2D. They're much more interesting than that, a 360 degree, five-senses experience across time.

Recommended books

Yes, books. They contain far more information than any website and don't break expensively when you drop the tablet/Kindle/phone in the greenhouse. And they don't need a wifi signal. You can even stand a tea mug on them.

General guides

RHS guides: As well as the massive 'Encyclopaedia of Gardening', the RHS has divided this into individual books on, for example, kitchen gardening, pruning, propagation etc. Clearly laid out and usually the most modern thinking on the topic.

The Pruning of Trees, Shrubs and Conifers, by George Brown, revised by Tony Kirkham. The pruning bible. if you have a garden with a lot of tees and shrubs, this really is chapter and verse on how, when and - perhaps most important of all - whether to prune.

Dr Hessayon 'Garden Expert' series These are the most popular gardening guides in the world. I am assured that there really is a Dr Hessayon and he does write them himself, otherwise you might assume a small factory somewhere.

These picture-books cum how-to guides cum quick reference books cover specific aspects of gardening in sharp, focussed detail.

If you want a book on roses, roses you shall have, with standardised photographs, categorised, described and mapped out in absolute and comparative terms. I have several and I suspect every gardener has at least one. (I know Christopher Lloyd did, they're in his library).

Fruit and Vegetables

Not really my forte, but books by Joy Larkcom and Carol Klein are practical, interesting, cover off-beat as well as traditional options and are well laid-out. James Wong is popularising Asian vegetables.

Orchard fruits are a major investment so you will need to study up on varieties, pollination partners and pruning techniques if you're into a community orchard, or a heritage orchard. Have a look at the East Malling Research Station website.

'Permaculture' is an interesting idea which depends heavily on tree cover. It is a system to produce food from permanent planting; look at the Permaculture Asssociation website for recommended books.

Also see the RHS guides and the 'Garden Expert' fruit and vegetable editions.

Reference books

The Hillier Manual of Tees and Shrubs The professional's guide to trees and shrubs is 'Bean' but this is now online-only and not easy to navigate, so for general purposes Hillier's is a good option.

The main guide as published has no pictures so you have to work out what the botanical jargon means, but it is very comprehensive. The sort of book you replace when a new edition comes out

Phillips and Rix: 'Roses', 'Shrubs', 'Trees' etc. Invaluable picture-books, because these photograph plants in season, and show them in comparison. So instead of a loving 'artistic' close-up of a camellia flower, you will see a page of a dozen or so laid out side by side, taken on the same day, with a size-scale. The bulb book shows the whole plant, so you can gauge how tall and how densely it will grow. The tree book includes outlines of the mature plant.

Details of how to grow plants are not full: these books were designed to be sold across the world so UK gardening conditions would not be relevant. But they do cover hardiness and details of the plant's natural habitat

Writers

Graham Stuart Thomas

His contribution to twentieth century gardens was immense, not least as the gardens advisor to the National Trust for many years.

His books are masterly and should be on every serious gardener's bookshelf. 'The Old Shrub Roses', 'Climbing Roses Old and New' and 'The New Shrub Roses' defined how people think of species and 'old' roses, and he was instrumental in creating the 'old rose' collection at Mottisfont Abbey, Hampshire.

His 'Perennial Garden Plants - The Modern Florilegium' is an exhaustive list of ornamental perennials worth growing in the UK, 'Colour in the Winter Garden' led the way on designing for this season. 'Ground Cover Plants' lists and debates all the major groups that can be used for this purpose.

And yet – His vision was austere, which did rub off on the National Trust in later years.

Beth Chatto

Her books on how she transformed a series of spoil-heaps in Essex, near Clacton, into one of the most advanced gardens in England are a must-read.

'The Dry Garden', 'The Damp Garden', her 'Garden Notebook' and her more recent books about the creation of her gravel garden were both practical and inspiring, but note that practice might have changed recently, e.g. on chemicals.

She had an artist's eye for the tiniest details of colour and form, but she was a hands-on gardener, who knows what it is like to stand with your back to the north wind in December planting a sapling into mud. Her gardens remain open under a trust.

Christopher Lloyd

Probably the most influential British garden writer of the twentieth century. I suspect he even beats Vita Sackville-West, she of Sissinghurst. Remember that he was not a garden designer. The outlines of his garden at Great Dixter near Rye in East Sussex were set out by Lutyens in 1912 and not altered to any great extent after.

His special genius was an eye for plants, a total commitment to growing them, a love for life and colour, and no respect for 'good taste' or the gardening conventions of the time.

His tongue is often in his cheek, his opinions are strong, spiky but wonderfully well argued. He wrote the reference book on clematis, but his greatest garden books are 'The Adventurous Gardener', 'The Well-Tempered Garden', and 'Garden Flowers'. He wrote a weekly column for many years for 'Country Life' and there are several collections of these pieces.

Great Dixter's gardens are now run by a charitable trust, headed by Fergus Garrett, as an educational centre as well as a visitor garden.

Afterword

I hope you didn't try to read the whole thing at one go: there's a lot of information here.

As with any craft, take it at your own pace, don't be afraid to try things out but if you find yourself getting irritated or impatient, stop.

Impatient people have accidents. Put that chainsaw down.

This can be the hobby of a lifetime. I won't go on about how good it is for you, because personally, I switch off when I'm told to do something for my own good.

I wanted to tell you about gardening because it's fun.

So, go and find out.

For contact about this book:
rosegreengardens@btinternet.com

Printed in Great Britain
by Amazon